The Little Miami Railroad
1836 ~ 1936

THE LITTLE MIAMI RAILROAD COMPANY
817 Dixie Terminal Building
Cincinnati, Ohio

ROBERT L. BLACK
PRESIDENT
EDGAR E. PINGER
SECRETARY AND TREASURER

January 31, 1940.

Dear Stockholder:

      The president of the Little Miami in 1936, its centennial year, first suggested that a historical sketch of the Company be written and sent to the stockholders. Lightly and little knowing, I undertook the job. In an endeavor to state the facts and to give them adequate expression, the pamphlet that was suggested has grown into a volume, and, what with research and rewriting, three years have passed. The book is published at last.

      It is not a prospectus nor a circular sent out pursuant to law. It is not a report for stockholders. It is not advertising. It is not even propaganda. And no part of the cost, except the postage, has been paid by the company.

      The Little Miami Railroad is a gift from me to you. In the words of the King in the Irish fairy story: "Shure, it costs nothin'; it's warth nothin'; so, put it in th' bag."

      Sincerely yours,

Robert L. Black

The Little Miami Railroad
1836 ~ 1936

Robert L. Black

Commonwealth Book Company
St. Martin, Ohio

Copyright © 1940 by Robert L. Black
Copyright © 2020 by Commonwealth Book Company, Inc.
Originally published in 1940 by Robert L. Black
All Rights Reserved
Printed in the United States of America

ISBN: 978-1-948986-25-0

Cover illustration: Bridge Over the Little Miami River at Miamiville. *Cincinnati, Columbus, Cleveland, and Erie Railroad Guide* (Columbus, OH: Ohio State Journal Co., 1854), p. 23

ACKNOWLEDGMENTS

MOST of the source material for this sketch has been found in the reports, minute books and records of the Little Miami; the many quotations from the Annual Reports are identified by numbers in parentheses. The stories of the railroads which, joined together, make up the great present-day systems, are so interlocked that one must know something about every road east of the Mississippi to understand about any other. It has also been necessary to keep the economic and political history of the nation in mind. The bibliography, if printed, would have been long.

Thanks for help graciously given are extended to Edgar E. Pinger, Secretary of The Little Miami Railroad Company; Robert Barnard, until recently General Agent and Superintendent of the Pennsylvania at Cincinnati; George J. Adams, Chief of Corporate Work of the Pennsylvania Railroad; George F. May, Secretary of the Baltimore & Ohio Railroad; the Auditor of State at Columbus, Ohio; Harry L. Clark of Xenia; Charles W. Baker of Cincinnati; and others too many to mention.

1836–1841

THE BEGINNINGS

THE outstanding achievements of the American people have been in discovering and developing means of inter-communication. Our forefathers colonized a vast, unknown continent; they faced, first, a thick mountain chain that ran from the St. Lawrence almost to the Gulf, and beyond, uncharted rivers, trackless forests, and plains stretching a thousand miles beyond the horizon to another mountain range. This challenge of immense distances they met with a mixture of common sense, resource and daring that we like to think is peculiarly American. The boats and wagons they brought along with them were adapted to new needs, and the very moment the steam engine came from England it was put to work turning wheels and paddles. Later on, Morse invented the telegraph and Bell the telephone; the Wright boys from Dayton, Ohio, were the first men ever to fly the air. The gasoline engine and the radio were discovered elsewhere, but they have been put to an everyday use which is not matched in any other country in the world. With ships and railroads, the telephone, automobiles and aeroplanes and the wireless, we in America carry freight untold billions of ton-miles, go faster than any other creature has ever moved, and send the written or the spoken word instantly to the ends of the earth. We have done much to show humanity how to overcome time and space.

WHAT WENT BEFORE

After the Revolutionary War, the people on the Atlantic coastal plain, increasing greatly in numbers, crowded up against the Appalachian barrier and started to trickle through the gaps toward more open lands. The winning of the boundless West began. Bison streets and Indian trails were worn down and widened into traces and the first of the wagon roads. In 1806, Jeremiah Morrow of Ohio introduced a bill in Congress to build a National Road from Washington to the Mississippi. It reached the Ohio river at Wheeling in 1817, and by 1825 had crossed the Ohio plains to Columbus and was headed due west as the crow flies through Indiana and Illinois. Settlers going out with their household goods passed livestock and produce to be marketed in the east. Twelve thousand six-horse Conestoga wagons arrived at Pittsburgh each year; the racket at the stopping places and at the taverns where the wagon-boys drank and danced and fought was said to be deafening. Gentlemen and ladies traveled elegantly in gayly-painted Concord coaches.

Traffic took to the water wherever the highway touched a river bank, especially if it happened to be a tributary of that natural thoroughfare, the Ohio river. Frontiersmen used birch-bark canoes or dugouts borrowed from the Indians; the pioneers that followed built rafts and flat boats, sometimes in a dry creek bed awaiting a freshet to float them off, and usually broken up for lumber when they had reached the end of the journey; and still later there were keel-boats which were poled or warped back up stream, or towed by gangs of men straining at the cordelle. Seven fullrigged ships, eleven brigs, six schooners and two gunboats were built by New Englanders at Marietta and drifted down the Ohio and Mississippi to sail around the world. Five years after the *Clermont* had feebly paddled up the Hudson River, Robert Fulton, in 1811, launched a sternwheel steamboat patterned after her, the *Orleans,* at Pittsburgh, made the trip to New Orleans in fourteen days' running time, and tried vainly to assert a monopoly. A canal around the Falls of the Ohio at Louisville was dug with Federal and private funds, so that after 1830 trips could be made without a change of boats. Fares for cabin passage including board from Pittsburgh to New Orleans were forty-five dollars, and deck passage about one-fourth of that. Unbelievable as it may seem, the tonnage of steamers on the Ohio and Mississippi river systems in 1834 added up to half the entire tonnage of the British empire on all the seven seas.

Short canals that joined the natural waterways were among the earliest public improvements of the New World. The Erie still stands as first and greatest of trunk canals. Chartered in 1792 to transport the immeasurable resources of the West coming in over the Great Lakes, the digging actually began after the War of 1812, and it was opened with a great celebration in 1825, four feet deep and 364 miles long from Buffalo to Albany. "It was," they used to say, "the longest canal in the world, constructed in the least time, with the least expense, and with the greatest public benefit."

This achievement touched off the "internal improvement craze" with a bang, and the buoyant Americans of the Middle West set to work to change their untamed prairies into a civilized empire overnight. DeWitt Clinton, governor of New York, loaned his canal engineers and persuaded John Jacob Astor in 1824 to buy $600,000 of the bonds issued by the state of Ohio for two waterways from Lake Erie to the Ohio river. He was on hand a year later with Henry Clay when Jeremiah Morrow, then governor of Ohio, broke ground at Middletown for the Miami and Erie canal. It was to connect with the Wabash canal at Defiance, and eventually in 1850 it reached Lake Erie at Toledo, 301 miles from Cincinnati. The other went through the center of the state from Cleveland to Portsmouth. In 1835, there were forty-eight canals in the United States, totaling 2,617 miles in length, and costing over a hundred million dollars.

Next came the railroad, faster than any horse-wagon and surer than any vessel navigating waters sometimes stormy and often icebound. Two years after the first rail was laid between Darlington and Stockbridge in England, granite for the Bunker Hill monument was hauled three miles by rail from Quincy to the Neponsett river, and anthracite coal was carried across Moosic mountain to the Delaware & Hudson canal. In 1829, just about the time George Stephenson was proving the usefulness of the steam locomotive to the British public in the Rain Hill tests, his *Stourbridge Lion* made a trial trip in Pennsylvania. Two years later, the first train ever drawn by a locomotive on the American continent ran from Albany to Schenectady. Baldwin began building engines in 1832 at Philadelphia.

Long before that, in 1823, John Stevens of Hoboken, aboriginal railroad inventor and pre-eminent of them all, secured a charter to build a "railed way" from Philadelphia to Columbia on the Susquehanna river, 81 miles away. For five years there was a lot of promotion but no construction whatsoever. Meantime, Philadelphia was beginning to lose first place to New York because of the Erie canal; and so the state of Pennsylvania took over the project in 1828 as a section of its Main Line of Public Works, which was starting, part rail and inclined planes but mostly canal, "in defiance of obstacles innumerable," westward on its way towards Pittsburgh. A double track to Columbia on the Susquehanna was opened on April 1, 1834, for privately owned cars drawn by horses.

Baltimore, in turn, was griped by the success of the Erie canal. Evan Thomas, who had seen the Stockbridge railroad in operation in England, stirred his friends up to organize the Baltimore & Ohio Railroad. They got subscriptions of three million dollars: a million, each, from the state, the city and the people. On Independence Day, 1828, Charles Carroll of Carrollton, sole surviving Signer, broke ground at the outskirts of Baltimore, and, in so doing, the fragile old man, ninety years old, said: "I consider this among the most important acts of my life; second only to signing the Declaration of Independence, if even second to that!" Twenty-five miles of double track were completed within a year and a half with iron strip imported from England, and in 1836 the trains were running over the "Y" Bridge into Harper's Ferry and had carried a total of over a hundred thousand passengers. At first, the cars were pulled by horses and even sails were tried out experimentally; but in 1836 the road had seven locomotives with vertical boilers, known as "Grasshoppers," thirty-four passenger coaches and a thousand freight cars.

About the same time down in the Carolinas, the cotton planters of Charleston, grown immensely wealthy since Eli Whitney had told them how to comb out the seed, and the industrial revolution in England had created an inexhaustible market, were building a road back through the plantations to Hamburg, opposite Augusta, at the head of navigation on the Savannah river. They paid the entire cost themselves without government help. Livestock and lumber were put aside to make way for cotton bales, and passenger fares were so low that no white man could afford to walk. The *Best Friend of the South*, said to have been built up out of discarded parts of the original *Stourbridge Lion*, ran off the rails and was wrecked on the first trip, in November, 1830. On June 17, 1831, the Charleston & Hamburg made an all-time first: a boiler blew up while a gentleman of color was sitting squat on the safety-valve.

Here and there other bits of railroad were starting out: the Mohawk & Hudson in 1831 between Albany and the end of the Erie canal; in 1832 the New York & Harlem, six miles long through New York City and the most expensive per mile ever constructed; in 1835, the roads from Boston to Providence; and so on. The Erie Railroad was chartered in 1832 with a capital of ten millions, to run from near New York across the southern tier of counties of the state, and thus redress a grievance against the Erie canal—although partisans of the canal kept saying it was chimerical and useless.

At the end of 1830, there were some thirty miles of track in the whole United States. In 1836, 1,273 miles were in use.

CINCINNATI, Queen City of the West, was the biggest town beyond the Alleghanies. The country between the two Miami rivers had been opened for settlement immediately after the Treaty of Greenville ended the menace of Indian massacre, and an influx of immigrants rolled in great waves over the Appalachians. This brought on a land boom, which in the inevitable course of events ended in a collapse, so that in 1819 Cincinnati was almost sold out to its creditors. But during the six years after 1830, that exuberant, boundless optimism, which, in cycles, inspires and then betrays the American people, began to swell up and up again to the bursting point.

1836 was the *annus mirabilis* of Cincinnati. The Ohio river and its tributaries are navigable for six thousand miles, the Tennessee and the Cumberland for thirteen hundred more, while the streams of the Missouri-Mississippi watershed are so many that their total length is past counting. A steamboat could reach at a hundred points into the passes of the Appalachian range, all through the raw Northwest up to the foot of the Rockies at Ft. Benton, and down to saltwater at New Orleans. Cincinnati rivaled Philadelphia, Baltimore and New York, and seemed destined to be the market place where the produce of the south and the west would be exchanged for the manufactures of the north and the east. For the moment, its business was largely in supplying foodstuffs to the southern plantations that had given up grains and gone over to cotton, exclusively; wholesale grocers in Cincinnati grew rich shipping the three great staples, flour, lard and whiskey, down the river. And in case of doubt as to whether whiskey was a necessity of life, witness the reply of the early Cincinnatian when asked how he could use two barrels in less than a month: "Hell, look here now, I've got a possel of children, and the cow's run dry."

The idea of building a railroad from the Great Lakes to the Gulf to serve the commerce of the immense territory between the Appalachian mountain range and the Mississippi sprang naturally in the minds of men feverishly engaged in traffic between the north and south.

As early as 1825 the people of Sandusky were talking of a road to follow a fur trader's trail through the woods to Dayton, and on New Year's day of 1832 they secured a charter for the Mad River & Lake Erie

Railroad. The first earth was turned in September with great festivities. A year or so later John C. Calhoun, beloved leader and spokesman of the South, voiced a demand that the line from Charleston be extended through to Cincinnati, and a committee was formed at Columbus under the leadership of William Henry Harrison to assist at the Ohio end. South Carolina, North Carolina and Tennessee willingly granted charters and money in aid. The legislature of Kentucky hesitated for a while, held in check by the jealousy of Louisville, but at last split even between the two by incorporating a Cincinnati, Louisville & Charleston railroad. This seemed to close the last gap. On receipt of the news, Cincinnati celebrated its joy with the firing of cannon, bonfires and a general illumination of the city. A small boy, little Edward Ferguson, who was later to be the driving force behind the Cincinnati Southern, remembered, all his life long, the glory of the candles shining in the windows through a snow storm and the February dusk. "From that time," he said, "I have been a Southern Railway man."

A Southwestern railroad convention was called at Knoxville in July of 1836, presided over by governor Hayne (of the Webster-Hayne debate) from South Carolina, and attended by delegates from Ohio, Indiana, Kentucky, Virginia, Tennessee, the Carolinas and Georgia. Resolutions calling for a road from Cincinnati, south through the bluegrass and over the Cumberland plateau to meet the Charleston road extended northwardly from Augusta, were adopted amid intense excitement.

THE LITTLE MIAMI RAILROAD COMPANY

Would the Queen City of the West in the pride of its brilliant youth hang back? Not so. The Little Miami was Cincinnati's answer to the challenge from Sandusky and the friendly hail of the South.

It was incorporated on March 11, 1836, by act of the General Assembly of Ohio; for until the adoption of a new constitution in 1852, every Ohio corporation, however conceived, was given birth by the legislature.

The charter bestowed powers to "construct and maintain a railway . . . commencing at any eligible point in or near the town of Springfield . . . thence by the most practical route through the town of Xenia . . . and down the valley of the Little Miami river and of the Ohio river to the city of Cincinnati;" and ". . . to make any contract with the Mad River and Lake Erie Railroad Company, either to unite in the construction of such parts of the road as may with propriety be common to both, or to provide for the joint transportation of burdens and passengers. . . ." The authorized capital stock was $750,000, divided into shares of $50 each, and commissioners were named in the counties along the line to receive subscriptions. The act required that directors be elected in eighteen months, that contracts for a quarter of the road be let within thirty months, and that the entire road be constructed within seven years.

The legislative fathers, of course, expected the Company to furnish vehicles and motive power, and

THE BEGINNINGS 15

they fixed the rates at five cents per ton-mile for freight and three cents a mile for passengers. It stuck in their minds, however, that a railroad was, after all, a sort of a super-turnpike, more up-to-date perhaps because of the rails and the locomotives, but, nevertheless, always open for use by the common people. To that end they provided that upon payment of tolls of one and one-half cents per mile, "all persons . . . may, with suitable and proper cars, transport persons and property on said railroad, subject to the rules and regulations of said company, as to the construction and speed of said cars, and the regulation of the motive power." In time the farmer, who on occasion hitched old Dobbin to a cart loaded with garden sass and wanted to trundle into town at three miles an hour, became too much of a nuisance. Ohio, in 1840, forbade any person to transport over the Little Miami without license from the president or directors. The Pennsylvania Railroad, however, waited six years longer for relief.

Those who may think that recapture and government ownership are something new and communistic should take note that the State reserved the right to buy in the entire works at cost, plus fifteen per cent, within thirty-five years, and to tax all dividends over six per cent.

Let Jeremiah Morrow stand here, as he stood from the very first, as the protagonist of the Little Miami. "The project was devised," he wrote in the First Annual Report, "of forming a railroad communication, connecting the lake and the Ohio river, and passing through the intermediate country between the two

State canals. For that purpose a charter was granted, incorporating the Mad River and Lake Erie Railroad Company. . . . At a subsequent period the Little Miami was incorporated, for the purpose of . . . connecting with the first mentioned road at the town of Springfield. . . . A continued railroad communication to the lake, simply considered as affording facility to travel between the West and the Eastern and Northern Atlantic States, would be of great advantage. But in a commercial point of view, the advantages are still more obvious, and the promise of increased trade to the city of Cincinnati cannot fail to enlist her commercial citizens in support of the enterprise. . . . With this channel open, much of the produce would be sent to and large supplies drawn from a Southern market." (I)

THE PIONEERS

There was need, in the creation and building of the Little Miami, for the imagination, courage and efforts of strong and farseeing leaders. Who and what manner of men were they?

JEREMIAH MORROW was foremost. He came of immigrant Scotch-Irish, and was born in 1771 on Maske Manor, near Gettysburg in Pennsylvania. Self-taught except for a most rudimentary education in the three R's, he left home at twenty-three and drifted into the Ohio country in the spring of 1795. He helped survey the Symmes Purchase between the two Miamis and the Virginia Military District, and

FROM A DAGUERREOTYPE
TAKEN AT LEBANON, ONE WEEK
BEFORE HIS DEATH.

finally settled on a farm near Foster's Crossing of the Little Miami river. There in 1812 he built a grist mill and a saw mill that became known to every farmer up and down the valley.

Austerity was the tenor of his personality; he held himself steadfastly to a rigid standard, and he forgave no slackness. His demands, however, were primarily upon himself, and the list of his works is long. He served in the Second Legislature of the Northwest Territory, the First Ohio Constitutional Convention of 1802 and in the State Senate, and was governor from 1822 to 1826. He devoted himself to the cause of the public schools. He was the first representative of Ohio in Congress, was re-elected four times and in 1813 became United States Senator. For sixteen succesive years he rode horseback to and from the sessions in Washington. He introduced the law that authorized settlers to buy the public domain at $1.25 per acre for homesteads, and thus was known as the father of the Federal Land System.

"No man, within the sphere in which he acted," Henry Clay said of him, "ever commanded, or deserved the implicit confidence of Congress more than Jeremiah Morrow."

The Little Miami could hardly have gone through without him, without his "well known and sterling honesty" and his influence on public opinion, and surely not without his determination and courage. He took no pay for ten years of hard work, except fifty-eight shares of stock, voted toward the end by the directors as "a small acknowledgment for his valuable services and expenses."

ORMSBY M. MITCHELL is a figure that still sparkles in the shadows of a hundred years ago. Born on a miserable pioneer Kentucky farm in 1809, he was taken to Lebanon, Ohio, and taught mathematics, Latin and Greek there in a school kept by his brother. Apprenticed to a storekeeper and maltreated, he ran away to be a wagon-boy. John McLean, later justice of the Supreme Court who lived in Dayton, got him an appointment to West Point. So in 1825 he put a knapsack on his back and twenty-five cents in his pocket and started off in a company of fur traders toward northern Ohio, was guided by an Indian to Sandusky, took passage on a lake-boat to Buffalo, trudged on foot to Lockport, worked his way along the Erie canal to Albany and down the Hudson river and landed at West Point still with twenty-five cents in his pocket. There he graduated in 1829, fifteenth in a class of fifty-six which included Robert E. Lee and Joe Johnston.

After serving for a time as an engineer loaned by the army to survey the B&O, he resigned and came to Cincinnati to practice law and to teach mathematics, philosophy and astronomy. He is remembered for the famous Cincinnati refracting telescope, which Noah Webster picked to illustrate the word "telescope" in the early editions of his dictionary. He raised $6,500 in 1842, a great sum for those days, went to Europe and ordered a twelve-inch object glass, magnifying up to 1400 times, from Merz of Munich. In 1845 it was mounted at the Cincinnati observatory and dedicated by President John Quincy Adams.

THE BEGINNINGS 19

In the Civil War he was rapidly promoted to Major-General and fought brilliantly in Tennessee, but Buell and Halleck hated him. Out of spite, they sent him down to Beaufort, South Carolina, to command a few Union troops and organize negro regiments. "I came to be buried," he said on arrival; and he died of yellow fever in two weeks.

He was a man of contradictions; his restless energy, hopefulness and supreme self-confidence took him a long way, but seemed to land him nowhere. Ormsby Mitchell, master-surveyor of the heavens and the earth, never made a true estimate of actual distances. He started and furthered enthusiasms for great projects, but he ended by stirring up a general ill-will. His motto was: "Ich ersteige"; so he did, but he always stumbled.

OTHERS who went along were:
Clark Williams, born in North Carolina of Quaker stock. A friend of Ormsby Mitchell, and in and out as secretary of the Little Miami, he was displaced in 1847 by John Kilgour, and moved to New York. Thereafter, the spellings: "carrs" and "nett," disappeared from the minute books.

Mathias Kugler came in 1797, a youthful emigrant from Baden, hatless and barefoot, it is said, to Little Germany, established by Chris Waldschmidt, leader of a band of Pietists fleeing persecution, in a bend of the Little Miami river just below Camp Dennison, married the daughter, and in time suceeded to the ownership, of the grist-, saw-, paper-, and oil-mills, the distillery and the general store. He subscribed $10,000 to the stock of the Little Miami on condition that the survey run within eighty rods of his mills.

John Hivling, an emigrant from Pennsylvania to Xenia in 1809, first a miller, then a hotel-keeper and wool merchant, in 1811 the last sheriff in Greene County to flog a criminal, and in his last years president of the Bank of Xenia and its leading citizen.

Major James Galloway, Jr., of Xenia, son of a Kentucky pioneer who settled in Ohio because he hated slavery. His aunt Rebecca was sought in marriage by the great Indian chief, Tecumseh. He grew up to be a surveyor, and fought in the River Raisin campaign during the War of 1812.

THE EARLY DAYS

The first meeting of the Little Miami was held on May 13, 1836, at Linton's Hotel in the small Quaker settlement of Waynesville, about half-way between Cincinnati and Springfield. Fourteen commissioners out of twenty-one came riding in on horseback from up and down the valley: among them, Robert W. Buchanan from Cincinnati, Mathias Kugler, Allen Wright of Lebanon, General R. D. Forsman, Hivling and Galloway of Xenia, and James Boyle down from Springfield. Resolutions were adopted to open books of subscription at the Firemen's Insurance Company in Cincinnati and at the offices and homes of the commissioners, for a period of six weeks beginning June second.

On that day, the commissioners met again in Xenia at Merrick's, a famous hotel of the time. Things had

THE BEGINNINGS 21

been slow during the hot summer and their job was continued six weeks longer, but with a "duty" to report subscriptions to Major Galloway in November.

The day of the underwriter of securities had not dawned, at least west of the Alleghanies. The commissioners could look in two directions only for subscriptions. First, there were the merchants, the mill owners and the neighborhood farmers, who had made money in the phenomenal prosperity of the closing days of the Jacksonian period and wanted to ship their goods. Second, the towns, townships and counties through which the road passed, and the state of Ohio which had chartered it, offered even more obvious possibilities.

During the winter the legislature authorized the city of Cincinnati to borrow $600,000, and to subscribe $200,000 to the Little Miami, $200,000 to the Cincinnati, Louisville & Charleston which was not yet organized, and $200,000 to the Whitewater canal connecting Cincinnati with the National Road in Indiana. Greene County, where Xenia is located, was given leave to subscribe $50,000.

Ohio had in 1835 received a loan of over two millions out of a thirty-seven million dollar surplus in the Federal Treasury, which was, for the moment, entirely free of debt. Thereupon the legislature "in order to diffuse the public patronage more generally and to benefit those sections of the State most remote from the Canals" on March 24, 1837, passed "an Act to authorize subscriptions to . . . Turnpike, Canal and Slackwater Navigation Companies," to the extent of $3,000,000 each year. It provided that "every Railroad company . . . to the capital stock of which there shall be subscribed an amount equal . . . to two-thirds of the estimated cost of the road and fixtures, shall be entitled to a loan of credit from the State . . . equal to one-third of the estimated cost of the road fixtures, to be delivered to the Company in negotiable scrip" whenever the two-thirds of the estimated cost had been spent on the right-of-way and on grading. The money was ear-marked for the purchase of rails and cars and engines. Each company must agree to pay the interest on the scrip and to pledge its tolls and profits to the State of Ohio for repayment of the sums advanced.

Things seemed hopeful when the commissioners met on May 3, 1837, at the office of the Firemen's Insurance Company in Cincinnati. Subscriptions "on a scale fully equalling previous anticipations" of "about" 1,680 shares were reported, and it was announced that Cincinnati and Greene County would come in for 5,000 shares, as soon as subscriptions from individuals reached 4,000. Ormsby Mitchell was in attendance and offered to make a reconnaissance survey on horseback from Xenia down the valley of the Little Miami river to Cincinnati for a thousand dollars. He was engaged at once and the subscription books were ordered to be kept open four months longer.

THE PANIC OF 1837 interposed. In the years just previous the country had gone mad, speculating in land and turnpikes, canals and railroads. Business men and farmers were so busy swapping future chances that they had no time to work in the counting rooms or to till the fields. One hundred forty-nine million dollars in unsecured and usually worthless bills, issued by Andrew Jackson's "pet" banks, were floating around. Then suddenly Jackson broke the back of the boom with the Specie Circular requiring payment for government lands in gold or silver, and laws were passed forbidding the circulation of bank-bills. European creditors immediately tried to cash in on their American securities and threw them on the market. New York, Philadelphia and Baltimore banks called their loans. The Federal government withdrew its deposits. Every bank suspended specie payments and most of them shut their doors. Out in Cincinnati there was a riot in front of the closed doors of the Ohio Life Insurance & Trust Company, and Ormsby Mitchell, undersized but dauntless, quelled a bloodthirsty mob by parading through it, alone, in his militia uniform.

1837 was the worst convulsion yet known. The breakdown was complete, and the nation lay prone for seven long years. No farmer had money to pay his debt. The factories closed, half the working people lost their jobs, and starving men paraded the streets. Let those who believe that the poor have never been so abused nor the rich so heartless as in Roosevelt days, read what a Cincinnatian, Moses Ranney, wrote to his wife from New York in 1840:

"I was up yesterday in the neighborhood of the Alms Houses, and a very large number of the most squalid and miserable looking human beings I ever saw white and black mingled together and mothers with their infants in their arms, waiting for their turn to get a ticket from the office for their *Weekly Allowance* of a shovel full of potatoes.

"Only think of it in this land of liberty and abundance. The earth groaning with an abundant harvest when so little is requisite to sustain life that there should be so much misery and suffering. With the hand of Charity extending the pitiful allowance of a shovel full of potatoes for a family's weekly subsistence, and then again to turn into the next street (Broadway) and observe the splendor and magnificence of the opulence of some and the *splendid misery* of others and contrast it with the scene I have just left. It made me sick of the place and its inhabitants."

At such a time it was next to impossible to get subscriptions from the people, and, however anxious the public authorities might be to help, the government had no credit. All the little roads that had sprouted before 1837 withered and died back to the roots, not to revive until the sun shone again in the Forties. Morrow and his forces still went doggedly ahead; their faith and steadfastness was put to the test and proven in these dismal days.

It was nothing less than amazing, in the face of the national disaster, that at a meeting of the commissioners called on August 4, subscriptions to 4,000 shares were announced. Mitchell had signatures for 800 shares and was thanked for his "zeal, industry and ability"; Major Galloway brought 233 from Xenia, and General Forsman 286 from the rest of Greene County; citizens of Cincinnati had subscribed 560 in small lots; and people in Clark County 186, on condition that the road should run through Clifton. The rest came scattering from the clearings in the woods up and down the Miami river. There were not quite enough of these to make up the entire amount needed, and so the list was padded with subscriptions for 302 shares from insiders, who were assured that they would not be called on to pay up and who were in fact, released from liability as soon as the required quota was reached.

It was now in order to call the shareholders together to elect directors. The meeting was held on August 23, 1837, at Dennison's Tavern in Cincinnati, and twelve directors, including Morrow, Galloway, Hivling, Buchanan and Kugler were chosen. George W. Neff, beloved Mayor of Cincinnati, "zealous advocate of every judicious project for the improvement of the city," was elected President. Because of other interests that might conflict, he thought it best to resign, but he remained always a faithful friend of the road and made the public and the politicians pay attention to its needs.

The next day, Morrow was elected to succeed Neff, and the Board proceeded to business. The route surveyed by Mitchell up the valley of the Little Miami river from Cincinnati to Springfield was approved, and he was asked to take charge as Engineer. The directors, then, by resolution, "deemed it expedient for the Company to apply for the benefit" of a Loan of Credit under the Ohio law. The first payment of five dollars per share on subscriptions was called.

At the meeting a month later, it was announced that the council of Cincinnati had appropriated

$200,000 to buy stock. The appointment of Mitchell was confirmed, his salary fixed at $2,500, and Clark Williams was named at four dollars a day to locate the road with the help of the President and the Engineer, and to obtain rights of way.

The three could not make a go of it, apparently because Mitchell stood out against the other two. He resigned in May, and a year or so later on the Company repurchased his stock and adjusted all his claims.

Robert H. Fontleroy was appointed to do the work over again, and to locate the twelve miles from the city out to the Little Miami river. His estimate of costs reported to the Board in August was just twice what Mitchell had figured. A committee to investigate this "discrepancy, so great as to cause mature deliberation," obviously did not know what to think. It saved face by reporting the next day: "A variety of circumstances have combined to retard the efficient commencement of the preparatory measures and the commencement of the work. . . . Whether any blame should be attached to anyone or, if so, to whom, it does not seem necessary to inquire, as it is believed more necessary to ascertain what is most proper now to be done than to indulge in useless regret at what has been done or what has been omitted."

The new Board, after the election of directors in September, backed Fontleroy against Mitchell, but without openly taking sides, and placed the road between Columbia and Kugler Mills under contract at a cost not to exceed $10,000 per mile. Morrow was authorized to negotiate for the use of the street along the river bank through the village of Fulton just east of the city limits. Elsewhere generally, rights of way were offered free of charge by owners who were glad enough to have the railroad run through their property. In a very few instances only, did exorbitant charges oblige the Company to resort to the condemnation proceedings authorized by the charter.

Fontleroy did not last much longer than Ormsby. On December 10, 1838, he was replaced by Robert M. Shoemaker who had had practical experience on the Mad River. The Board ordered him to locate the line from Xenia to Springfield.

That winter everything slowed down for lack of cash. In March, 1839, the council of Cincinnati, seemingly in hope that it might somehow wriggle out of its subscription for stock, put the Board on the rack with an inquiry as to when the road would be finished. "We are grateful," the directors replied with a sort of hollow sweetness, "to find that the City Council retain their friendly feelings toward the road, assured that it will lead them to an early arrangement for the payment of their stock, and the more so, as many individuals decline making subscriptions or meeting their installments. . . . until the Directors entitle themselves to payment from the City and obtain it. . . . The prospects for a speedy completion are more flattering than when the City made its subscription. . . . It is no longer a question whether it is proper to commence the work, as one quarter of the entire line is under contract and at an average of about 15% below the estimates, and about Ten Thousand Dollars of the said work already done and the balance progressing rapidly."

The President carried the bluff along by announcing to council the next day that Division No. 1 from the corporation line of Cincinnati to Columbia had been placed under contract, and that a committee of Directors would meet soon with council to fix a point of termination in the city.

Council, not to be outplayed, also made a gracious gesture. On May 6, it authorized $60,000 of bonds to be issued in part payment of its subscription. However, it stopped right there and held on tight to its money; it did not hand over one penny's worth of bonds.

In September, 1839, the Board was told that 8,307 shares had been subscribed; 5,000 by Greene County and Cincinnati, and 3,307 by individuals; but that, in spite of three calls and every effort to collect, $32,796 only, or less than eight per cent had been paid in cash on subscriptions during the last three years.

Things had come almost to a standstill. The state of Ohio, which a year or so before had pretended to play Santa Claus to every little child of a railroad, suddenly turned Shylock, and exacted, in addition to a first lien on all properties, a "writing obligatory" making directors personally liable for interest and principal on every Loan of Credit. It was just as bad outside Ohio. Even the Baltimore & Ohio, with many millions invested in its road and in more or less successful operation since 1830, was not able to sell a single share of its stock in this country or in England.

THE BEGINNINGS

A CHANGE toward prosperity was at hand. John Kilgour, senior partner in the wholesale firm of Kilgour & Taylor, came to the rescue in the crisis with a loan of $7,665, and Greene County put up $12,000 on the security of the personal endorsements of the directors. Eight months later, the State actually turned over $40,000 in six per cent bonds on account of the Loan of Credit.

The very next week, contracts were let for lumber for the superstructure of fifteen miles to Kugler Mills, near Milford. In September of 1840, Cincinnati paid three-tenths of its subscription by the delivery of $60,000 in six per cent bonds payable after 1850. A contract for the "graduation" of ten miles of the road-bed above Kugler Mills was made, and Shoemaker, the engineer, was ordered to "repair" to New York and Philadelphia to bargain for strip-iron rails and a locomotive engine.

A review of finances on April 29, 1841, when the outdoor building season was starting, showed that $195,539 altogether including another $25,000 from the State of Ohio had been collected, while $59,691 had been spent on construction, $12,195 for rights of way, and $9,316 in interest on the Ohio and Cincinnati bonds. Bills payable ran up to $28,915.

Things began to hum. Twenty thousand Ohio bonds were sold at a discount to Baring Brothers in London and the proceeds used to pay for railroad iron shipped from England. A contract for enough more to finish another ten miles was authorized. Arrangements were made to use part of the Columbia & Goshen turnpike running out from Cincinnati toward the Little Miami river. Council offered first an entrance to the city which might be revoked on six months' notice, but was persuaded to grant a permanent right of way over Front Street from the corporation line to Deer creek, on the express condition that no locomotive should ever be admitted to the tracks. Shoemaker was appointed Chief Engineer for three years, and Clark Williams was told to stand ready to go to New York or even to Europe, if necessary, to get iron for seventy miles of track. A passenger car had been bought during the winter for $487.59. A four-wheeled twelve-ton locomotive, built by Rogers, Ketchum & Grosvenor of Paterson, New Jersey, which cost $7,000 plus $730 for water carriage via New Orleans, was delivered in July, 1841. It was about ten feet long and of course had no cab, so that the engineer stood in his stove-pipe hat on a bare platform and took the sparks and the weather as they came. Twenty Cincinnati bonds were traded in for a depot site and a river landing 500 feet front on the Ohio river.

At the end of 1841, the Engineer reported to the Board that the road from Cincinnati to Milford was open to traffic; that the grading from Morrow's Mills, just below Foster's Crossing, was completed and ready for rail; that Lonergan, the contractor, was prosecuting with much energy, the grading for ten miles above Morrow's Mills, "fully sustaining his high reputation for ability and perseverance"; and that the contract for lumber had been extended to Todd's Fork, thirty-five miles from Cincinnati and the iron ordered.

CINCINNATI IN 1841.

MIAMI CANAL IN FOREGROUND;
OHIO RIVER AND KENTUCKY HILLS IN BACKGROUND.

THE BEGINNINGS 31

The cost of 14.13 miles of finished line was $10,-517.50 per mile, a total of $148,611—about $13,000 less than Shoemaker's estimate.

THE SUPERSTRUCTURE of the Little Miami conformed to the best design then in use. The first track of the Baltimore & Ohio had been laid in 1827 on granite blocks set corner to corner, and even in 1839 the rails of the Utica line rested on piles driven twenty feet down in the ground. The engineers of the Little Miami, however, used cross-ties of wood, which, as John Stevens of Hoboken had discovered in 1831, give just the proper combination of play and firmness, and which have never been bettered by any other kind of construction. These oak ties, six inches square by eight feet, were placed at first on top of the loam or clay of the roadbed, but later were imbedded in gravel and sand and still later in stone ballast. The supply of virgin lumber was inexhaustible. Only iron was scarce in that early industrial day. And so the rails were stringers of white oak twelve feet long keyed to the ties, with strips of iron for the wheels to run on, three-quarters of an inch thick and two and one-half inches wide, spiked down at the inner edge of the rails.

Of all stupidities, the diversity of railroad gauges in America would seem the most hopeless. No one has ever been able to explain why Stephenson, who designed the first English locomotive, pitched on the queer axle-length of four feet, eight and one-half inches. However, so it was, and quite naturally and properly England, and in turn the Pennsylvania Main

Line of Works, the Baltimore & Ohio, the Virginia Central, and the other early Eastern roads, as well as Kentucky, Indiana and Illinois, followed suit. The Delaware & Hudson, however, chose four foot-three, the Wilton Road in New Hampshire four-seven, the Mohawk & Hudson four-nine, the Lake Erie & Louisville four-nine-and-a-half, the Camden & Amboy in New Jersey four-ten, the South Carolina and all the other southern roads until after the Civil War five feet even, and the Erie with its affiliates a boasted six feet. The *Sandusky*, first locomotive to run in Ohio, delivered to the Mad River road in July, 1838, was four feet, ten inches in width. The story goes that the directors were so entranced with its and their own glory, that, even though no track had been laid, they fired up and blew the whistle for hours and hours. If so, the echoes lasted long, for the legislature passed an act which made any gauge except four foot-ten unlawful in Ohio.

Sectional jealousies, attempts to bolster up local monopolies and inertia perpetuated the muddle until it had caused an infinite amount of delay, annoyance and expense. Usually passengers and freight had to be unloaded, carted across town and then reloaded. Sometimes a third rail was laid down inside or outside the regular tracks, or else the cars were lifted off bodily by steam hoists and set down on other trucks. It was estimated that a break in gauge cost as much as to run a train fifty miles further. Only after long years, the original English standard of four-eight-and-a-half, which experts say is really too narrow for economical operation, became standard throughout the world.

THE BEGINNINGS

TRAFFIC

CONNECTIONS with the Little Miami did not exist in 1841, because there were no other railroads in southwestern Ohio. The Cincinnati, Louisville & Charleston lay at rest forever. The Mad River & Lake Erie, like the Little Miami, had survived, but feebly; construction was started in September, 1835, and in 1841 sixteen miles from Sandusky to Bellevue was passable.

Cincinnati was more on the lips of men, however, than any other city in the land; St. Louis was a mere trading village and Chicago a frontier post. Its population was 46,388 in 1840 with 33,783 more living in Hamilton County. Along the Little Miami fifty-four flour mills were making 100,000 pounds of flour each year, and there were twenty-six saw-mills and three paper mills, at Plainville, Milford, Germany, Indian Ripple, Polktown and higher up. The Ohio river traffic was booming; in one year, 1840, thirty-three new river boats, aggregating 5,631 in tonnage and $592,500 in cost, were launched from the ways in Cincinnati boat yards. Forty to sixty coaches ran daily to and from Springfield. Business for the Little Miami would not be lacking if ever it should be finished.

THE FIRST TRAIN passed over the road on December 14, 1841. City council and a large number of citizens were invited to take the initial trip from Fulton to Milford. It consisted of a brand-new locomotive christened the *Governor Morrow*, a "brigade" made up of the *James Madison,* a thirty-passenger compartment coach (that is, sixteen inside and fourteen, including the guard, overhead in fine weather) the *Little Miami,* a twenty-passenger side-seat car, and a freight car or so. It left Fulton at 11:00 o'clock of an overcast morning, but was delayed by a fall of earth across the track. This served only to prove the power of the *Governor Morrow,* and the train none the less reached Milford safely in an hour and a half. While the distinguished guests tarried over lunch, the townspeople were taken for a short excursion on the rails. The return trip to Fulton was made in the extraordinary time of less than an hour.

"We felt strongly," the Cincinnati Gazette said the next day, "as we were whirled along at a rapid pace, what a change a few years had caused in this glorious West. All honor to the enterprize of the people who can work such wonderful changes." Please do not think the puffing little train and the enthusiastic little reporter wholly ridiculous. That trip was the end to which men like Morrow had fought without let-up through seven long, hard years.

"This work," Strader reflected in after years, "advanced from a small beginning, struggling against want of money, credit, of confidence upon the part of the public, and embarrassed by the novelty of the enterprise and the inexperience of all connected with it." (VI)

1842–1850

STRUGGLE AND STRENGTH

THE LITTLE MIAMI was bankrupt in 1842; in 1850 it was known throughout the country as "the model road."

PERSONNEL

During the Forties the leaders changed one by one. Those who had first picked up the burden were replaced by younger men who had served their apprenticeship. Jeremiah Morrow held on until 1848 and resigned his post only "when the infirmities of age rendered him incapable of performing its duties." (VI)

"The fabric is worn out," said the world-weary old man, "My associates are nearly all gone. I am acting with another generation. . . . I feel I am in the way of younger men."

JACOB STRADER, Treasurer of the road from 1844, succeeded Morrow. Born in 1795, a New Jersey farm-boy, he was brought at twenty-one to Cincinnati by his kinsman, John H. Piatt, and employed in the family bank. He proved too stout a fellow to work indoors, and in a year or so took to the river as a steamboat clerk on Cincinnati's first steamboat, the *General Pike,* a stern-wheeler of the U. S. Mail Line, thirty-one hours from Louisville to Maysville. In 1822 he was captain of the boat. He built a second *General Pike,* a sidewheeler, in 1824, and two years later the *Ben Franklin,* familiarly called "White Chimney Ben," and founded the Cincinnati & Louisville Packet Line which came to have ten boats in daily service. Altogether, he owned twenty-three steamboats and he ran them prudently and prosperously. After he took up with the Little Miami, he stayed ashore, but he remained always deeply interested in the river. He was also president of the Commercial Bank, and founded an immense factory 380 feet long at Third and John Streets in Cincinnati to fabricate the cotton taken in exchange for food sent to the South.

No man was more admirably fitted in mind and temper to give to the Little Miami what it needed most. He had that sense of teamwork which made men glad to work with him; he had a pioneer's spirit of fairplay and helpfulness toward his neighbors; he had the resolute will that brings a sailor over uncharted waters to a distant port; and he had a sturdy, enthusiastic, truly American belief in the goodness of his countrymen, his city, and his own business.

"I consider," he said once in a statement of his philosophy, "all competition to be salutary, and tending to the prosperity of these different corporations, who will be impelled by it to do better service to the public, and thus secure more permanently their own interests, than they would otherwise be induced to do. And it may be added, that such rivalship though salutary, must exert itself more in appearance than in fact; for the construction of all these roads must in-

crease the business, the products, the wealth, and the population of the country, and each one, by adding to the general prosperity, will benefit all the others. There will be business enough for them all, and we ask only for the Little Miami Railroad, that reasonable portion of it which will be fairly attracted by the location and character of our road, the comfort, speed and safety of our trains, and the convenience of the public." (VII)

"We feel it due to justice and gratitude," his Directors said when in 1857 he refused reelection as President, "to put on record for perpetual reference our testimony to the lasting obligation under which Captain Strader has placed the stockholders, and our deep sense of the kindness, frankness and cordiality which have characterized his deportment and our strong attachment to him personally, and our earnest desire for his welfare."

Upon his death on April 6, 1860, they spoke once more of his "high character, inflexible integrity, great business talents and indefatigable industry"; and ended: "In all things he was a model of what is just and right."

JOHN KILGOUR went on the Board in 1842. He immigrated from Bristol, England, and came to Cincinnati in 1818. In the booming days that followed the depression of 1819, he and Griffin Taylor formed a wholesale grocery firm trading with the South that came to own its own fleet of steamboats. The concern was dissolved in 1840, for no other reason than that the partners had become rich enough.

Kilgour built the fine mansion on Third Street overlooking the terminus of the Little Miami and the Ohio river that is in use today as a Marine Hospital.

He had common sense, that clear realization of facts in their true bearings, the bulldog grit of the Britisher, and an insight into the right value and use of money. He served on almost every committee appointed by the Little Miami Board, was its Secretary and for one year its President. When he died in 1858, he was a large bondholder and one of its largest stockholders.

ROBERT M. SHOEMAKER was born at German Flats in New York. At nineteen he was a forward-chainman on the Erie canal and later he surveyed in Canada and along the Lake Shore. In the fall of 1837, he reached Sandusky to become engineer of the Mad River. The next year Morrow begged him away for the Little Miami. After four years he returned to his former job, and from 1849 to 1852 he was building the CH&D and after 1854, the Covington & Lexington. He raised the money from his own friends to finish the Dayton & Michigan and threw his entire fortune into it. He was the kind of outdoor man who builds railroads, not on paper in an office, but, in fact, on the ground.

OTHERS, one by one, slipped into the seats of the original directors as they were emptied. Abraham Hivling replaced his father in the Bank of Xenia and on the Little Miami and lasted there thirty years, serving most of the time as a director of the Columbus & Xenia also. John Kugler, the son, succeeded Mathias.

THE UNKNOWN MANY—headed by the conductor, the "captain of the Brigade" in a frock coat, choker collar and stove-pipe hat, who was half clerk, half guard, with a dash of the gentleman, and drew more salary than the president of the road—all played their parts well. "We employ none but temperate, capable men and we tolerate no disobedience or neglect of duty," said Strader, "It is a pleasing part of our duty to remark upon the correctness and good order which have attended the management of our trains and depots. Great care has been taken in the selection of Conductors, Engineers, Clerks, and other Agents, to employ capable persons, of good habits, and civil deportment, and to require of them, care, attention, and punctuality in the discharge of their duties, as well as to be uniformly civil and obliging to passengers, and persons transacting business with us in any form. We believe, that in this respect, our Road has been very fortunate. Our trains are conducted prudently, and with the most careful regard to the safety of our trains, and the comfort of travelers." (VII)

FINANCING AND BUILDING

1842 broke dark and dismal, with a "derangement of the currency," to use Jeremiah Morrow's words, "a stagnation of commerce and a consequent depression in the price of produce." Fifty thousand dollars in Ohio six per cent bonds, the last of the Loan of

Credit from the state, were used in January to pay for work done on the four divisions of the road under contract. In February the Little Miami had $2,300 in cash to pay $7,500 due to contractors and it would cost $99,000 to finish the road to Todd's Fork. The Little Miami implored its subscribers to pay the last twenty dollars per share.

On April 6th there was a showdown. At the morning session of the Board, the Treasurer reported debts of $116,013 and "means" (that is, unpaid balances of individual, city and county subscriptions to stock) estimated at $110,000. The directors worried throughout the day, and had their supper. "Met at Candlelight" so begin the minutes of the adjourned meeting. You can see old Jeremiah Morrow, in the soft light of those candles that guttered out a hundred years ago, looking grimly around the table at his disheartened followers. They had nothing to suggest. Finally, young Kugler moved to mortgage, as security for the loan long past due to the Bank of Xenia, the *Governor Morrow*, three passenger and eleven freight "carrs," five bay horses with five sets of harness, the office furniture and all the railroad iron and lumber on hand not permanently laid down on the road, with the right to use the road as far as finished and to apply the "nett receipts to the extinguishment of the debt." Next they voted to stop all work in progress and to place in the hands of Robert M. Shoemaker, as commissioner, all the contracts and negotiations and all the means and stock of the Company.

During the spring and summer Shoemaker sent out collectors to hound delinquent subscribers, but there was small substance left in any purse after five lean and hungry years. He did succeed in borrowing $10,000 from the great New York firm of Winslow, Lanier & Company, hypothecating $20,000 of Ohio bonds, and he divided the proceeds up in small sums to meet the most urgent demands of contractors and creditors.

John Kilgour was elected a director in the fall. Hard-headed, downright and experienced, he took the floor at the first meeting of the new board and moved the appointment of a committee: "first to ascertain the entire sum paid in by shareholders and the State of Ohio and from other sources; second, to investigate the disbursements of whatsoever kind to whom, by whom, and what for; third, to ascertain the amount due from the stockholders, and, if practicable, to specify what can be made out of unpaid stock; fourth, to ascertain sums due by the Company, to whom owing, what for, and when payable; and fifth, to investigate conditions of the contracts existing and report in reference to their being continued or suspended."

The report made a week or so later was a bitter dose to take. First: $89,973 had been collected from individuals, but of this $30,555 was in notes, not in cash. Greene County, Cincinnati and the State had paid $332,000 on their subscriptions. The Company had received to date, including $7,488 from operations, a grand total of $429,462. Second: $416,072 had been spent on construction and equipment, and $51,533 on real estate. Costs of operation were $6,263, leaving a modest profit of about twelve hundred dollars.

Third: Individual subscribers still owed $57,694, but $32,176 was "bad and doubtful." Cincinnati and the State had paid up everything they had promised and there was still $32,000 due from Greene County though "not yet available." Fourth: The Company owed $51,482 on notes, balances due contractors and judgments.

Construction, nevertheless, still went forward. "In preparing the line of the road for grading," Morrow explained later, "it was struck into short sections, to enable industrious men with small means to become contractors, and to insure a more certain fulfillment of the contracts." (II) This was smart business, because a little fellow puts a small job through and rests content a long time on a promise to be paid as soon as possible; whereas the big man wants cash on demand or he stops the work. Thus the fourteen miles beyond Milford including the bridge across the Little Miami river just above Camp Dennison were finished and put in use on December 1, 1842.

Up to that point the valley is broad and level, but it narrows beyond, and the only approaches are down steep ravines that lead from the table-land on either side. A mile or so above Governor Morrow's grist mill, near Foster's, the river turns sharply to the east for nine miles before it reverses northwardly again. Both Mitchell and Shoemaker had run surveys from Deerfield (now King's Mills) up Turtle creek through the proud little town of Lebanon, to re-enter the valley further up at Waynesville. The feeble little locomotives of the day, however, balked at grades of thirty-three feet to the mile, and the engineers thought best to stick to the gentle slope of the valley along the river bank.

In the spring of 1843 a party of the first citizens of Lebanon rode down to Morrow's Mill and in their best manner laid a request for a branch road before the Governor. The old gentleman gave them dinner and horse-feed, and promised to present their claims to the Board. This he did without fail, but the other directors after thinking it over refused to do aything about it.

It seems clear from hindsight that they made a mistake. The road through Lebanon would have run on a straight line through a smiling and thickly-settled countryside instead of twisting around curves in a gorge, which mid-way, at Fort Ancient, is three hundred feet deep. With two trains daily the saving in distance would have been 7,300 miles a year. And finally the management of the Little Miami would have avoided the headaches caused by the intrigues of the angry Lebanonites.

On March 13, 1843, the legislature, which the year before had suspended the Loan of Credit Act, plugged the spigot for good and all. Over the whole country, a hundred millions of government funds had been spent on canals and railroads during the period of the internal improvement craze. The taxes to pay the bonds could be collected only with the greatest difficulty from hard-run and disgusted property owners, and a violent popular reaction set in against Public Works. Some states were even forced to the last humiliation of repudiating their debts.

The politicians, of course, had backed the wrong horse and put fourteen million dollars into the Ohio canals, just as the national administration today has committed itself to water power as against steam-generated electricity. And the politicians, with the old time-honored technique, tried to turn attention away from their blunder by leading an attack upon the railroads. The Ohio legislature, for instance, passed an act requiring the Columbus & Xenia to pay the Canal Commissioners, in case their revenues should be diminished by any diversion of traffic to the railroad, one-half of the tolls that might have been charged by the canal. Strader, who rarely missed a trick, took pains in his 1846 Treasurer's Report to forestall an impending raid: "It is gratifying to find, that while our receipts are large, no portion of them are taken from the public works belonging to the State. . . . The region of the Little Miami is too distant . . . to come into competition with them in the transportation of heavy articles. . . . The road . . . instead of interfering with the State revenue, will be the means of adding to it, by enhancing the value of taxable property, bringing active capital into the country, increasing population, and stimulating business." Even the Pennsylvania, with all of its influence in its own legislature, was not relieved until 1861 of a penalty of half a cent per ton of freight carried by the road between December and May when the waterways were frozen shut.

Ohio contributed $717,515 to six different railroads under the Loan of Credit Act. With the sole outstanding exception of the $115,000 in Little

Miami stock, which paid dividends and was sold at a handsome profit in 1862, every cent put into railroad stocks was lost. It is not surprising that the new Ohio constitution adopted in 1852 forbade the state and all lesser governmental subdivisions to make loans or subscriptions to any kind of company.

"The Little Miami Railroad Company," said Morrow, as fair-minded a man as ever lived, "was entitled to the benefit of the provisions of this act, and the Directors availed themselves of the portion of the loan they were entitled to under the law, while it remained in force. . . .

"The withdrawal of the proffered means, on which, in part, the Company had predicated their contracts, was highly disastrous. They had been made in good faith and in firm reliance on the plighted faith of the State. . . . The Directors . . . duly appreciating the consequent embarrassment . . . resolved that the contracts then in the course of execution should be suspended or where practicable, with the consent of the parties, annulled. . . ." (1)

It was the darkest hour of the Little Miami. At the next meeting of the Board Shoemaker reported that urgent measures were indispensable to squeeze the money out of private subscribers, and that notes for some five thousand dollars he had received were so doubtful that no creditor would take them in payment. The Directors authorized him to mortgage anything the Company might own for a temporary loan. Instead, he threw up his job in despair.

On July 1, 1843, the entire property was assigned to William Lewis, Esq., of Fulton, in trust for two years and then to be sold for the "extinguishment" of any debts remaining unpaid. Even doughty old Jeremiah Morrow seemed to lose hope for the first time in so many years.

"The money expended in the work partially executed and abandoned is unproductive, and the work done suffering dilapidation. . . . The fund already invested is but little better than dead capital . . .," he explained to his stockholders, "To the contractors who had finished their jobs, and no means on hand to pay their just dues, notes on the Company bearing interest at six per cent were given. The Company at this time labored under great embarrassment and found it impossible to realize funds from property and stockholders in time to meet the pressing demands of creditors. Numerous executions against them were in the hands of the officers, and the machinery necessary for the daily working of the Road was levied upon, and in one or two instances sold. These claims were for small amounts, before magistrates, and on trial, it was found impracticable, to settle them except by making payment in cash. After giving the subject a careful consideration, it was determined, as a measure of justice to the remaining creditors of the Company, to place the Road and all its fixtures in the hands of a Trustee. A contrary course would have prostrated the work and have been the cause of much injustice." (I)

Immediately after the assignment a mob of tough Irish laborers, brandishing picks and shovels and howling for their wages, besieged the Lewis house in Fulton, but he appeased them by butchering cattle, which the farmers had turned in on their subscriptions, and distributing the meat.

There followed the lull that often comes between an act of bankruptcy and the day when the vultures crowd in to pick the bones. The demands of the most pressing creditors were met by the sale of part of the land on Front street in Cincinnati, purchased for the depot. The summer and fall passed.

"There is little ground for discouragement as to further progress," said Morrow at the end of the year with forced cheerfulness, "or despondency as to final completion in due time. The debts are manageable. . . . The property possessed should thence be of equal value with the expenditure by which it was produced." (I)

In February the legislature extended the time for the building of the road five years longer and increased the capital stock to one million dollars. Then, in April, Cincinnati voted overwhelmingly for a loan of a hundred thousand of six per cent bonds payable on December 31, 1880. The Little Miami issued its own bonds to the City payable on the same day, pledged the net proceeds of the road to pay interest, and mortgaged the tracks, the engine, the cars, and all other property, with a power of attorney to confess judgment. Eighty thousand dollars of Cincinnati bonds and $23,000 of Greene County bonds were delivered and sold in July, and Clarke County, where Springfield is located, subscribed $34,000 for stock. The road was completed to Morrow.

For, after seven gloomy years, the sun was, at last, shining again. Polk had been elected president and

, the excitement and easy money of the Mexican war were just around the corner. In a few years, California would pour a flood of gold into the treasuries of the world. A returning tide of commerce had set in. The American people were getting ready once more to believe that their resources in materials, money and mind would never be exhausted, and that there would never be any limit to their destiny.

Both Morrow and Strader knew that the unwholesome practice of begging money from the government was at an end. However, the handlers of money were again willing to take another chance on railroad ventures. As early as 1843, Ormsby Mitchell, who always seemed to be the forerunner, had suggested getting stock subscriptions in the east. He was given two hundred dollars for traveling expenses, but the time was not yet ripe and he brought nothing back.

Early in 1845, the question as to where the line north of Xenia, on its way to Springfield and junction with the Mad River, should be located, was up for final decision. The original survey followed the valley of the Little Miami eastwardly through Clifton. Due north across the gently rolling upland was Yellow Springs, and there lived brisk and enterprising William Mills, its proprietor and the founder with Horace Mann of Antioch College. He offered to get money in the East without remuneration and to pay his own expenses, granted that the road might go through his little town. The engineers found that a mile and a half in distance and a considerable amount of the cost of construction could be saved, and the legislature, by act passed March, 1845, authorized a relocation, provided that all subscriptions were paid back to the people living along the line that had been abandoned. The Board "after a personal view on the ground . . . with great unanimity expressed a preference to the line passing by the Yellow Springs." The citizens of Clifton brought suit and raised legal questions "such, perhaps," to quote Morrow, "as are only intelligible to persons learned in the science of the law." (III) But without success.

William Mills was duly appointed agent to negotiate a loan for the Little Miami, and this he succeeded in doing in Boston, largely through the support of Nathan Hale, editor of the *Daily Advertiser*. The Little Miami issued, as of May 1, 1845, $200,000 of seven per cent bonds payable on May 1, 1855, and secured by mortgage to William Sturgis and Josiah Quincy, Jr., of Boston and Timothy Walker of Cincinnati, junior to the lien for the Cincinnati bonds. The bondholders had the privilege of surrendering any bond for twenty shares of stock within nine and the Little Miami of paying off within five years. The terms of the loan were considered too onerous by the Little Miami directors, except that "a continuance of the work, then in progress, to its final completion . . . and an early connection with the Mad River and Lake Erie Railroad . . . were deemed sufficient to justify the Company in the acceptance of the loan. . . ." (III)

The line to Xenia was opened for regular business in August, 1845. "The embarrassment arising from inadequate means provided for the construction of the work has now, in a great measure, been overcome . . .," said Morrow at the end of the year, "The work is now approaching its completion; but a few months more and the line of road up to its terminus will be brought into profitable use." (III)

True to this promise, the first train of cars passed over the road from Cincinnati to Springfield on August 10, 1846.

"There is not," said Morrow, "strictly speaking, an acre of waste land, on the whole line—no spot which cannot be made useful, in some way—and by far the greater portion unequalled in point of fertility. The number of mills dependent on the road, to a greater or less extent, for the transportation of their manufactures, averages one to the mile, and it is the opinion of one well qualified to judge, that the business of Springfield and its neighborhood, will yield a larger revenue to the road than is now realized from the road south of Xenia." (III)

The advances in the art and the increase in the use of the line were both so great, however, that even before the building was barely done, rebuilding began. "A road structure too light to sustain the weight and wear of heavy trains in ordinary times," Morrow said in 1847 in his last Annual Report, "could not be kept in good order, or even passable condition, without constant attention and a heavy outlay. . . . At the time of the commencement of our Road, the means for construction were but limited; works of the kind were new to the country . . . the estimates of cost and the capital stock designated by the Charter were all calculated on the scale for a cheap work. . . .

The Road was made to conform to the measure of the means provided, and was formed with light plate bar iron, the mode then in common use. It was soon discovered that roads formed on this construction could only be safely used by running at a slow speed, and with a light train." (V)

For instance, the first six miles out of Cincinnati had been laid on the irregular surface of East Front street and the Wooster turnpike. These were narrow, up-and-down thoroughfares, constantly thronged with wagons and carriages. Near the city the layers of greasy clay, characteristic of the Silurian Uplift, slid with every heavy rain out of the overhanging river bluffs and constantly encroached on the tracks. The location of the line was finally moved from the streets to its own right of way nearer the river.

Then, as the flimsy superstructure decayed and racked apart—"four years is the extent of time that we can rely on the best white oak" (IV)—the iron strips had a nasty way of springing up and raking the underside of the cars. There was much talk during the Forties about the new-fangled "T" or " ⊥ " rail, a model of which James Stevens had whittled out of wood while on an ocean voyage, five years before the Frenchman, Vignolles, claimed to have invented it. Four thousand tons, sixty-one pounds to the yard, were bought for the Little Miami in 1847, and five thousand tons more in 1850.

"The original flat bar has now been removed, and the T rail laid down on forty-seven miles of the road between Cincinnati and Xenia," Strader stated proudly in the Report for 1850, "leaving but seventeen miles to be improved. Previous to putting down the heavy rail, the track has been repaired, and in many places reconstructed, the grades have been reduced, the road straightened, the bridges repaired, and the waterways enlarged. All this work has been done in the most substantial manner and with a view to permanency, so that when the remainder of the road shall be relaid in the same way our road will compare favorably, in construction and durability, with the best railroads in the United States. . . . The remainder of our road . . . also will be relaid . . . without delay, and with such improvements as may be found necessary. . . . Our road will then offer inducements to the traveler which will probably not be surpassed elsewhere." (VIII)

The Board wanted to finance the entire cost with its own shares, and an application for an increase of stock was made to the General Assembly early in 1847. The authority was granted, but subject to provisos that, the Mexican war being then in full swing, the governor should fix charges for transporting all troops and munitions, and that the legislature might prescribe all other rates for passengers and freight, if deemed too high. This was a primeval move toward regulation, and Morrow, a rugged individualist, if nothing else, would not even call a meeting of his stockholders to discuss it. Instead he spoke out in his last Annual Report, the Fifth.

"On the principles of just policy," he said, "the public authorities ought to aid and foster the exertions of associated individual enterprise, in the construction of improvements so eminently calculated to promote the general prosperity and wealth in the community. . . . We then have a reasonable confidence that the application of our Company to the Legislature, will be favorably received—the capital stock of the Company so enlarged, as to enable them to complete the work in which they are engaged. . . ."

No politician had the backbone to withstand the indignation of the venerable Jeremiah Morrow, and the capital stock was extended to three millions at the next session.

The directors adopted that wholesome practice of ploughing the earnings back into the business, which, until lately when unsound and excessive taxation has wiped out all surplus, has done more than any other thing for the creation of American wealth. The stockholders were content to receive between 1845 and 1850, forty-nine per cent in stock dividends, thereby increasing their original investment by half.

"The remainder of the profits," Strader recommended in 1848, "should be carefully and diligently applied to the improvement of the road—to the erection of permanent bridges and depots, to giving width and solidity to the embankments—strength, durability and safety to the tracks—to the purchase of superior machinery and cars." (VI)

"It will be expedient to continue the policy," he went on at the end of 1850, "which has heretofore been pursued with good results, of expending the earnings of the Road in its completion, and making our dividends in stock. The mode first named has this advantage; that we borrow from our own stockholders and avoid the payment of extravagant premiums for money. By this mode we invite our stockholders to use their own money, to enhance the value of their own property, and to secure a future revenue from capital already invested; and by keeping down the pecuniary liabilities of the Company, we sustain its credit. On the other hand, if we attempt to raise large sums of money by offering either our bonds or our stock in the market . . . we should make such sales under great disadvantages, and at a heavy discount." (VIII)

When the cash ran short, the balance was borrowed on short-term unsecured bonds, convertible into stock. These were, in fact, little more than promissory notes which the Company expected to pay out of earnings, or, if the creditor chose, they became subscriptions to stock at par. As the road grew to be more and more profitable, most of the bonds were converted, and the money thus saved was also used to expand the business.

For those who find comfort in figures, the following tables are inserted:

CAPITAL STOCK

Year	Authorized	Outstanding	Dividends
1842	3/11/36: $750,000		
1843		$431,124	
	$119,000 issued to State of Ohio for a Loan of Credit.		
1844	2/5/34: $1,000,000	$471,936	
1845		$549,245	3% in stock
	$50,000 issued to Greene County, and $25,000 to Clark County.		

Year	Authorized	Outstanding	Dividends
1846		$ 584,830	3½% in stock
1847		$ 632,601	5% in stock
1848	2/24/48: $3,000,000	$ 740,523	8½% in stock
	All delinquent stock subscriptions foreclosed by sale.		
1849		$1,146,314	10% in stock
1850		$1,418,875	10% in stock

Loans

Issue	Principal Amount	Rate	Security	Redemption or Conversion into Stock
Cincinnati Loan, due 1880 ...	$100,000	6%	First Mortgage on earnings and assets	1880: $100,000
Eastern Loan of 1845, due 1855 ...	$204,390	7%	Second Mortgage on assets	1848: $ 4,390 1850: $ 10,000
Loan Bonds of 1846, due 1856	$119,000 in 1846 $101,000 in 1847 ——— $220,000	6%	None	1848: $ 80,000 1849: $ 57,000 1850: $ 22,000
Loan Bonds of 1848, due 1858	1848: $ 82,000 1849: $ 8,000 1850: $110,000 ——— $200,000	7%	None	
Collateral Bonds of 1850 ...	$165,000	6%	None	

The total capital investment of the Little Miami in December, 1850, was $2,130,627, and this had been spent, in part, for construction, $1,650,673; for depots, etc., $168,664; and for machinery, $311,290.

The total cost of the eighty-three and one half miles of road was $25,874 per mile. The Baltimore & Ohio built 186 miles for $54,283 per mile; the Boston & Lowell spent $70,751, and the Boston & Worcester, $71,394. Because of the integrity of Morrow and Strader, and Clement, its engineer, the Little Miami cost was the lowest of any except that of the Charleston road, which was built, 213 miles, with slave labor for the amazingly low figure of $16,766 per mile.

DEPOTS, ENGINES AND SO ON

The first passenger station was a frame building, twenty by twenty-four feet, two stories high, built on land under perpetual lease on the river bank east of Deer Creek just below the old Cincinnati water works.

Warehousing the freight moving in and out of the city or being transhipped to and from the steamboats was, however, more important than pleasing the passengers, who seemed to accept cheerfully whatever discomfort traveling might involve. The station was, therefore, devoted to freight in 1844. Two other fireproof brick depots, 294 by 54 feet and 250 by 40 feet, were required within two years afterward to handle the load. Meantime, the passengers were given a small frame building of "a temporary character."

At Xenia, James Gowdy settled a row as to where the road should run, by donating his house and lot on

Detroit Street, just one block from the courthouse square, for a depot. This exactly suited John Hivling; his wool warehouse was just across the street, and his hotel, his bank and his store, in the next block above on the same side. It is a legend that he built a platform over the tracks so that travelers stepped off the train right at the hotel-desk. In 1850, a "large and convenient brick station," which is still extant, was erected at the junction of the Little Miami and the Columbus & Xenia.

LOCOMOTIVES were now getting to be a little more impressive. They weighed as much as eighteen-and-a-half tons, and the designers had evolved cabs to protect the eyes of the engineers from sparks and their stove-pipe hats from the weather. The fuel was wood, of course. Brakemen lived up to the name and actually swung on the brake handles at the end of each car. Each locomotive had a distinct personality and its own particular name—the *General Harrison*, the *Arthur St. Clair*, the *Shawnee* or the *Reindeer*—and a whistle so different from the others that everybody along the line knew it.

"There comes the *Buckeye*—I heared her toot," the schoolboys would yell, and tear away for the depot to see the train and the biggest engine on the road go by.

SPEED was a matter of pious horror to the God-fearing and of deep concern to the thoughtful in those days. Even the eight miles per hour attained in a pinch by the stage coaches from Utica to Albany was thought reckless. In 1828, the School Board of

Lancaster, Ohio, refused to countenance a debate as to whether railroads were practical and added: "If God had designed that his intelligent creatures should travel at a frightful rate of fifteen miles an hour, by steam, he would have told it through his holy pamphlet. It is a device of Satan to lead immortal souls down to Hell."

"The folly of people going fifteen miles an hour in railroad carriages," said Lord Broughham, urbane but still severe, "exceeds belief. They will pay a dear price."

"Till we have bones of brass or iron, or better methods of protecting them than we have now," such was the considered judgment of the scientific, "it is preposterous to talk of traveling fifty or sixty miles an hour as a practicable thing."

Facing so deadly a danger the city fathers could not, in the due exercise of prudence, allow locomotives to enter the precincts of Cincinnati. Accordingly, the engines were uncoupled and the cars hauled to the station by the bay horses that were mortgaged to the Bank of Xenia at the Candlelight meeting. The ban was not lifted until 1845, and then the speed was limited to four miles an hour so that a man could, if necessary, outwalk any train.

"Since that time," Clement, the Superintendent, was happy to say in his report to the Directors, "the trains have been brought in without the aid of horsepower; a result long desired; effecting a great saving in time and expense to the Company, and working no injury, it is believed, to the residents on the street." (III)

ENGRAVED VIGNETTE
ON STOCK CERTIFICATE OF THE FORTIES.

(*Note:* Apparently, the young couple are racing the train; the old gentleman would rather walk and get home for supper.)

Toward the end of the Forties, trains on the Little Miami averaged sixteen miles per hour from Cincinnati to Springfield, including the delivery of mail from the Post Office to the depot. "I do not entertain a doubt," said Clement, "but that, if it should be desirable, a speed for 'through' trains of thirty miles per hour can be got up and maintained with safety to passengers and a proper regard to economy. . . ." (VII)

Speed such as this brought with it an appalling slaughter of live stock. In the days of the flat-bar rail, the stolid cow or the corpulent pig would most certainly derail the engine, and it was the better part of valor to stop dead and chase them off the tracks. As soon as the new T-rail and the heavier engines gave more stability with far greater speed, the engineer stormed along with his hand on the whistle cord, and his faith in the cow-catcher, that highly practical and truly American device invented by Isaac Dripps, mechanic on the Camden & Amboy.

"Three accidents of a serious nature to machinery have happened," said Clement in 1849, "in consequence of running over cattle, involving an expenditure of nearly $2,500. . . . I would suggest the propriety of continuing to fence until the entire line is enclosed."

THE TELEGRAPH came in as the cars went faster. Train-dispatching in the early days was simple. The first engineer to reach a center post had the right of way, and the rule was that the other fellow had to back up to a turn-out. Sometimes, so the story goes, the crews fought it out, hand to hand. When a regular passing station was appointed, every one invited his soul in leisure until the meeting train came down the line. The modern block-system got off to an early start in the form of a dark brother roosting in a crow's-nest up a tall tree, who kept watch and signalled when the track was clear.

"Arrangements are now being made for the construction of a line of telegraph along our track," said Strader in 1848, just four years after Morse had staged his demonstration on the Baltimore and Ohio, "The wires, being constantly under the eye and care of the police of the Road, will to some extent be protected, and can always be speedily repaired in case of injury; while the dangers of Rail Road traveling can be greatly reduced by frequent communications from one station to another, the business of the Road facilitated, and the convenience of the passengers promoted." (VI)

CONNECTIONS

In the latter half of the decade, railroad building began in real earnest. The river trade between Cincinnati and the South, which had held more or less steady even in the worst times, began to boom.

THE MAD RIVER & LAKE ERIE seemed, in 1842, of the first importance both as a feeder and an outlet.

"This line," said Morrow, "will form a direct communication between the two great streams of travel on the Ohio and the lakes. Offering to the traveling public, a choice of routes to the sea-board, by a cheap and speedy conveyance, and to the merchant and business man, a medium of transportation open at all seasons of the year. The city of Cincinnati will also have the benefit of a daily intercourse with the extensive and fertile district of country bordering the lakes, and her commercial citizens be enabled to interchange commodities with a section of country, shut out for one-third of the year from any and every market by ice and snow.

"The time required to reach Boston from Cincinnati, during the season of navigation on the lakes, and after the opening of this line, will be less than three days, allowing for all reasonable contingencies." (III)

The Little Miami was assured in 1843 that the Mad River was making "strong exertions to push forward their work," and that they would soon finish their line; but two years later their Directors and Principal Engineer promised "that their road will be completed against the first of October next, so that in autumn the line will be open for business between the Ohio river and the lakes." (III)

Committees from both roads met to select suitable grounds for the Junction depot in Springfield, and arranged to put up a building, at common expense, on the south side, opposite to the center of the town, "for the reception and accommodation of passengers." It was agreed that the trains should run with a "continuity of the cars" and without change of freight and passengers, and that a joint ticket office should be opened on the Public Landing at the foot of Broadway where the steamboats landed in Cincinnati.

The Mad River people had leaned heavily on government aid to finance the road. The state had granted a Loan of Credit of $270,000, much more than to any other company, and the counties, townships and towns through which it ran furnished most of the rest of the money. When the Loan of Credit act was repealed and other public funds exhausted, however, there was nobody like Morrow or Kilgour or Strader to drive ahead with nothing except their own courage and persistence. The Mad River lagged behind and failed to keep its tryst at Springfield even after the Little Miami began to run trains into the Junction depot. As late as the summer of 1848, a distance of fourteen miles of the Mad River remained unfinished, "over which wagons and stage coaches were employed, upon a road not macadamized, and subject to become very heavy in wet weather," and caused "unavoidable delays, and sometimes annoying difficulties, which tended to turn the through travel off of our Road into other channels." (VI) It was not until 1849 that the road—"the nearest and most rapid channel connecting the Ohio and the lakes"—came into "fair operation."

Nothing then could restore the years the locust had eaten. While the Mad River was stuck midway on the plains of Ohio, other channels of traffic were forming. "The Mad River line . . .," said Strader in 1850, gracious, of course, and yet a bit haughty in manner "will continue to be an important road, notwithstanding the opening of other roads to the East, and to Lake Erie. . . . It will have advantages . . . in relation to the intercourse between Cincinnati and the Upper Lakes which is now becoming considerable, and will be yet greatly extended. . . . I am happy to say that our intercourse with them has been of the most harmonious and satisfactory character." (VIII)

THE COLUMBUS & XENIA, and not the Mad River, was destined to carry the line of the Little Miami toward the northwest. Chartered by the legislature on March 12, 1844, with a capital stock of $500,000, only Major James Galloway, Jr., who was named in the act as one of its commissioners, seemed to be a point of contact with the Little Miami.

An attempt was made by the new company in 1845 to start work at Columbus, but it fell a victim to the money famine. Then in 1847, succor came with a rush. Columbus and Franklin County subscribed $50,000 apiece, Madison County $20,000, and Xenia and Greene County together $56,000. Along with them the Little Miami appeared.

"The Directors, impressed with the importance of a Rail Road communication with the seat of Government, and a connection there with other Rail Roads to be constructed, promising greater facilities to Eastern travel . . .," said Morrow at the end of 1847, "have concluded an arrangement with the Columbus and Xenia Rail Road Company . . . for constructing a branch of their Rail Road from the town of Xenia through the County of Greene. . . . This branch road, when completed, . . . is to be transferred to the Columbus and Xenia, and thence become a part of their Rail Road . . ., the Little Miami having received an amount of the stock of the other Company, equal at par value to the cost of making this branch Rail Road." (V)

The Little Miami spent $362,050, which the C&X repaid with its shares in 1852. Other subscriptions came easily, and with the proceeds of $300,000 ten-year seven per cent bonds sold in 1849, the work continued rapidly from either ends at once over the gently rolling terrain of central Ohio. The process of railroad making had improved, and the engineers loaned by the Little Miami had learned much in their years of active experience. They laid the best T-rail available, 61 pounds to the yard, and they built an "uncommonly fine road, and one which might be run over with great speed and safety."

"The fourteen miles of this road, connecting with our road at Xenia, and extending thence to the Greene County line," Strader, whose work had been to prolong the road that Morrow had built through a wilderness, said in December, 1849, "were made during this year by our Company, and form part of our Stock. The whole line from Xenia to Columbus is now nearly finished, and will be ready for the passage of trains over it about the first of January. We may fairly expect a considerable increase of business. . . between the political capital of our State and the commercial metropolis, the more especially as Columbus is a very beautiful and prosperous city, offering, in addition to its valuable trade, many attractions to the traveler, and being the center of a great variety of roads and traveling facilities. . . ." (VII)

"The continuation of the same great line, by the

Cleveland and Columbus Company . . .," he continued at the end of the next year after the C&X had been in operation for ten months, "cannot be otherwise than productive of a greatly increased intercourse between these places, while both of them must receive large accessions of business, from a line traversing the width of the whole state, passing over a vast country of unrivalled fertility and resources, and uniting the navigable waters of the Great Lakes with those of the Ohio and Mississippi." (VIII)

THE HOPE OF A SOUTHERN CONNECTION still lived. The Charleston and Savannah roads had penetrated into the hinterland as far as Knoxville in 1839 looking for northern supplies and foods. A line through Kentucky starting at Covington just across the river from Cincinnati and running to Lexington was projected in 1847.

"This will be a very beneficial road to Cincinnati," said Strader, "and the other cities which will be connected by it, and to that fine region of country which it will penetrate. Our intercourse with that part of Kentucky is already very large, although our purchases consist chiefly of hogs, beef-cattle, and sheep, which are driven on foot to our market; but it will, on the opening of this road, embrace the various products of agriculture, while a new outlet will be found for our manufactures and foreign merchandise. The travel from Lexington will not be inconsiderable; but this road derives a great additional interest, from the probability of its extension southwardly through Kentucky and Tennessee, until it shall unite with that fine system of railroads which is now in rapid progress between Charleston, South Carolina, and Nashville, and by which we shall be brought into the great line of Southern travel—a continuous line from Lake Erie to the Atlantic Ocean." (VII)

While scanning the southern horizon the management caught a glimpse of other activities beyond the mountains. The Virginia Central, which had started in 1836, as the Louisa Railroad, from the Potomac toward the Blue Ridge mountains, was by 1850 in Richmond at one end and at the other almost at Charlottesville. It was in the mind of its engineer, Claude Crozet, father of West Point and of the Virginia Military Institute, to push through the gaps in the Blue Ridge with slave labor and so on to the Ohio river, but this did not come to pass until thirty years or more later, when the Chesapeake & Ohio came into existence.

"The distance from Cincinnati to Richmond, by this road, will be five hundred and sixty miles," said Strader, to whom nothing seemed impossible, "making a shorter connection between our city and the seaboard of the Atlantic, than any now in existence. . . . It is the first work of this kind, traversing the entire breadth of the great state of Virginia, and giving to her citizens direct access to the western states lying contiguous, and more nearly adjacent to her than to the more northern states. . . . It will open mineral regions of exhaustless wealth and of great variety, whose fertilizing streams will flow to the Atlantic coast, and to the shores of the Ohio. Its southern latitude will at some seasons give it advantages over the more northern routes." (VIII)

A DAYTON & XENIA road, paralleling sixteen miles of much frequented highway, was incorporated in 1846, and the Dayton & Western was organized in the same year by the people of Dayton, "one of the most beautiful and prosperous cities of Ohio," and of the "rich, populous and industrious country around it," to prolong the line west to the Indiana boundary. The Directors of the Little Miami offered to build half of the road from Xenia to Dayton, as they had done for the C&X, and to make a survey as soon as $20,000 was subscribed. Desire, however, outran performance and in 1849 the Little Miami was forced to contract for a line of stages running from Dayton through Bellbrook and down Sugar creek to Spring Valley, just south of Xenia.

The Dayton & Western, in 1850, heartened by a subscription of $50,000 from Preble County, was nearing Richmond, Indiana.

THE HILLSBORO & CINCINNATI was chartered on March 2, 1846, with a capital stock of $300,000 to build across the level upland eastward from the little town of Hillsboro and down O'Banion creek to intersect the Little Miami at Loveland, twenty-three miles from Cincinnati. The year before "the spirit of enterprise had awakened" in certain citizens of Parkersburg, in western Virginia, and they had organized a million-dollar company to extend the line of a hoped for branch of the B&O from the Ohio river across the lower part of the state to Cincinnati. The Hillsboro & Cincinnati expected to intercept this road at Chillicothe. It might seem to some that a mere clearing in the woods was giving itself airs in planning to become a great railroad center. Hillsboro, indeed, was still so primitive that, according to a little boy who later became United States senator, he and the other kids wore flour sacks for shirts and had to tie their chewing tobacco around their necks because flour sacks are never made with pockets. Those, however, who would sneer at the vain-glory of a tiny Ohio village, should bethink themselves that, a few years later, the Women's Christian Temperance Union was started in Hillsboro, spread in every direction country-wide, and brought on the disaster of national prohibition.

In any case, the city of Cincinnati loaned $100,000 of her bonds, the authorized capital was raised to $900,000, and the stock was promptly subscribed. By 1850, thirty-seven miles from Hillsboro to Loveland was finished, and a committee was appointed by the Little Miami to arrange for running its machinery over the new road, and for carrying the passengers and freight to and from Loveland.

"This," said Strader, "will be the shortest route between Cincinnati and Baltimore, and will be a formidable competitor with other roads for a share of the travel across the mountains. After leaving our road, it passes through a productive country, until it enters the Scioto valley, one of the finest districts of the State, containing a substantial population, and abounding in all the staples of our country. . . . Crossing the Scioto river at Chillicothe, about one hundred miles from Cincinnati, it passes on twenty-six miles further, into a rich mineral region, abounding in coal and iron of the best quality. These minerals are said to lie in a strata of great thickness, jutting out upon the valley through which the railway will pass." (VIII)

IN NORTHERN OHIO, between 1846 and 1850, bits of railway were eagerly thrusting out like shoots of the wild-grape. The flourishing city of Cleveland offset Sandusky and its Mad River road by reviving the charter of the Cleveland, Columbus & Cincinnati, granted in 1836 but dormant from non-use. Three millions of stock were subscribed, directors elected, surveys and estimates made, and by 1850 the road was in operation to Crestline, "and the remainder in a state of considerable forwardness" in winding along toward the terminus of the C&X.

In 1849, the Ohio & Pennsylvania started at Mansfield toward Pittsburgh. The Pennsylvania organized a three-million-dollar company with the same name to run west from Pittsburgh, and began taking subscriptions from the counties along the way. The next year, the Ohio & Indiana was incorporated to build west from the line of the CC&C through Bucyrus to meet an extension from Indianapolis.

"It cannot be doubted," said Strader, "that a continuous system of railways which shall afford a speedy transit for passengers from the seaboard to the principal city of the west, will be of great public utility, and profitable to all the roads which shall be united as links in the chain." (VIII)

Further south, the Steubenville & Indiana began in 1850 the construction of a road to run eventually by way of Newark and Coshocton between Pittsburgh and the C&X at Columbus. The Central Ohio connecting the B&O at Wheeling with Columbus was also in contemplation.

IN THE WEST, ever since Ormsby Mitchell made a look-see survey in 1836, the Ohio and Mississippi had lain dormant. The truth was that the river boats abundantly satisfied, for the time being, every need of transportation. In 1848, a company was incorporated in Indiana and in Ohio in 1849. Mitchell was hired to make another preliminary survey from Cincinnati to St. Louis and estimated the cost of the entire road at $5,045,390. The citizens of Cincinnati sanctioned a contribution of a million dollars in 1850, and City Council agreed to lend six hundred thousand of it for immediate construction. Illinois, however, thinking it had little to gain and fearing that the traffic from the west, just starting to go through Chicago, might be diverted to St. Louis, would not grant a right of way and in 1850 still refused a charter.

THE EASTERN SYSTEMS, meanwhile, reached eagerly toward the West. Somehow the management of the Little Miami did not seem to be sufficiently aware of them as to comment on their progress in the meetings of Directors or in the annual reports. The Baltimore & Ohio was carrying passengers in

November, 1842, to Cumberland, and transferring them to stage-coaches on the National Road. A dividend of thirty-seven and one half cents per share had been paid in 1831, and throughout the decade it kept on paying more or less regularly in cash or in its own bonds. But there it stood, facing the mountains and the appalling task of breaking through, and pondering whether to head, as first planned, for the Ohio at Wheeling, or to strike it at Pittsburgh.

The Main Line of Public Works of the State of Pennsylvania ran trains in 1842 over eighty-one miles of double track from Philadelphia to Columbia. A packet-boat on the canal, extending up the Susquehanna and Juniata valleys, 172 miles long, took the passengers to Hollidaysburg at the backbone of the Alleghanies. There it was taken apart, and hauled in sections across viaducts, through a tunnel and up five inclines by stationary engines, 1,398 feet in ten miles, to Blair's Gap Summit, and lowered down five planes on the side, 1,172 feet in twenty-six and a half miles, to Johnstown. When reassembled, the barge poked along 104 miles further to Pittsburgh. The entire trip took four weary days and nights; and it was no wonder the Main Line of Works failed to attract much through business.

In 1845, the B&O suddenly made up its mind to put out a six-mile branch from Cumberland to the Pennsylvania line, and prevailed on the legislature to grant Letters Patent for an extension to Pittsburgh. At this, Philadelphia instantly declared war, and a savage political battle ended on April 13, 1846, with the incorporation of The Pennsylvania Railroad Company on the understanding that if within a year $3,-000,000 were raised and contracts let for thirty miles of road, the grant to the B&O should lapse. Samuel Vaughan Merritt, intimately identified with the commercial and industrial interests of the city, was elected president and roused his fellow Philadelphians to such a pitch of exasperation, that subscriptions were solicited from house to house, and 1,800 people bought from twenty-five up to two hundred and fifty dollars worth of stock, each. The B&O thereupon gave up the fight and ordered Benjamin H. Latrobe, outstanding among the best of American railroad engineers, to survey the two hundred miles of line to Wheeling. The work of construction, which was not to end for five years longer, began in 1848.

Ground on the Pennsylvania Railroad was broken by J. Edgar Thompson on April 9, 1847, at Harrisburg. Two years later, the line from Lancaster to Harrisburg, owned by James Buchanan, was leased. In October, 1850, track was being laid in the Juniata valley half way to the Portage Road, and trains were running from Philadelphia over the state railroad to Lancaster and as far along to the west as Lewistown.

The Erie, did not get a start until 1835, and during the Forties was in and out of the troubles that checkered its career throughout. When it was placed in the hands of assignees for the first time in 1842, not more than forty-six miles of track, leading from the long pier at Tappan Slote on the west side of the Hudson, three hours' sail up from New York, was ready for the trains, and only 11,627 passengers and 5,779 tons of freight had been carried in six long years.

As soon as the financial skies cleared a bit, the legislature came to the rescue once more and forgave a loan of $3,000,000, while the stockholders were asked to surrender half of their stock. Three millions of new shares were subscribed and three millions of new bonds issued. By the end of 1850, 337 miles had been built and equipped at the awful cost of almost $21,000,000.

The New York Central did not as yet exist, and, even though after 1847 a passenger could entrain at Buffalo for Albany, he traveled over ten little independent bits of railroad. The Harlem Railroad was halted at the outskirts of New York, and the Hudson River Railroad had barely started up the East bank in 1847. The trip from Albany to New York was made, perforce, by steamboat. At the other end, beyond the western boundary of New York, a road from the town of Erie eastwardly was incorporated in Pennsylvania in 1842, the Cleveland, Painesville & Ashtabula in Ohio in 1849, and the Buffalo & State Line in 1850.

THE CH&D (to take sides in the feud at once, since this story of the Little Miami is frankly partisan) lay like a serpent in the egg until 1848. It had been originally incorporated at half a million in 1846 under the name of the Cincinnati & Hamilton, to emerge from the west side of Cincinnati and follow the valleys of Mill creek and the Big Miami river.

In July, 1848, S. S. L'Hommedieu, who came of a strong-minded Huguenot breed, gave up publishing the *Cincinnati Gazette,* and took the presidency. The name of the road was changed to the Cincinnati,

Hamilton & Dayton, and the legislature authorized an increase of the capital stock to one million. No aid was asked from any city, township or county. Instead, L'Hommedieu inspired such confidence that the citizens of Cincinnati raised $750,000 in three weeks, and $250,000 of bonds were sold in New York. This was clean and quick financing, almost without parallel in railroad history; for the Americans habitually turn to the government when in distress for money —witness the present Federal bureaus in aid of practically everything.

The Little Miami did not at first recognize the new road as a danger. "There will be other roads made, and various channels of commerce opened," Strader explained, "which will increase our business, without adding greatly to our expenses. Other railroads are not to be considered as rivals, but as auxiliaries; all that can be made in Ohio for years to come, will increase the general prosperity of the country, in a greater degree than they can take business from each other. We see no prospect that can diminish our receipts, but we see many that will swell them." (VI)

Construction went forward with record speed. Grading a road bed along the two broad valleys was easy; one stretch even went 45.3 miles without a curve. The weather was unusually dry in 1848 and 1849, so that there were few delays. Later, however, it turned out that the work had been too hastily done to stand up under heavy traffic, and the bills for repairs, as a result, were excessive.

It soon became obvious that the CH & D would go beyond Hamilton, but Strader and the rest of them still felt so sure of the everlasting supremacy of the Little Miami that they could find no reason to worry.

"The Cincinnati and Hamilton Railroad," said Strader in 1849, "passing out of our city on its western side, and proceeding up the valley of the Great Miami over a country of unsurpassed fertility, thickly settled, and highly improved, and having its terminus at a town possessed of inexhaustible water power, and other advantages for manufacturing—commences its career with the most flattering prospects. . . . Whether this road will be extended in the direction of Indianapolis, with a view of connecting our city with that prosperous capital, and swelling our commerce with the immense agricultural resources of that productive region, or northwardly to Dayton, and the fine country around and beyond it, is, I believe, not yet decided. It may ultimately take both these directions. Should the road be completed to Dayton, and thus become connected with Springfield, with the Mad River Road, it may fairly be expected to divide with us the business coming over that road. . . . On the one hand we shall be prepared for competition, on the other, the vast resources of the country, and their rapid increase, will, I am confident, not only furnish full employment to both roads, but tax the energies of both to their utmost capacity." (VII)

TRAFFIC

At the end of each year, the management reported the state of the business to its stockholders—Morrow speaking gravely, Strader with hearty good cheer, and Clement, the engineer, dryly and matter of fact.

1842. $904.71 was collected from passengers and $338.27 for freight during the first forty days of operations. We are competing with heavy teams long in operation on the turnpikes, and until disposition can be made of the surplus horses, wagons, etc., etc., many persons will be prevented from using the railroad. A better acquaintance with the many advantages it presents over the ordinary mode will eventually transfer the whole business to the line. Total collections were $6,981.35 and net income $3,189.31 —not so bad for fourteen miles of track.

1843. Twenty-eight miles are now in daily use. The passenger train departs at 10:00 A.M., and on the return trip leaves Foster's Crossing at 3:00 in the afternoon, Milford at 4:00; fare, one way: sixty-two and one half cents. The general depression and stagnant commerce are causes of embarrassment in the affairs of the Company. But "the indications of returning prosperity are strongly marked on every day transactions in the community. . . . Renovated confidence will succeed the late prostration." (I) $9,912.49 was taken in, but we earned a clear profit of only $3,043.92.

1844. The fund arising from the proceeds of the road has been satisfactory and equal to the expectation of all concerned and is constantly on the increase. Since the road was finished to Todd's Fork, a double train of cars has been run, and has met with full employment. Another engine, two 8-wheel and one 4-wheel "carrs," enough to carry 144 passengers at once, with eight 8-wheel and twelve 4-wheel freight-vans have been added to rolling stock. We carried

21,286 passengers all told and earned $18,632. Expenses were less than half of that. Not a single individual has been injured in life or limb.

1845. The foreign demand for breadstuffs and the abundant supply which can be afforded from the bountiful crops of the last harvest must turn the balance of trade largely in favor of our country. A steady increase of business has been realised in both passengers and freight. The motive power has been strengthened by the receipt of three engines. We made three times as much as last year and a net profit of $15,486. This will admit of our first dividend.

1846. The produce along the Rail Road has increased beyond our means of transportation, and has been accumulating at all the depots. It has not sought a market through other channels, but continued to flow into our depots, and there to remain waiting until the Rail Road can furnish conveyance. The insufficiency of machinery to do the business that offered has caused much anxiety and unpleasant feeling to those having charge of the management; it was overworked and soon out of order. The collision of August 13th rendered useless for two months the only effective passengers' engines. The Board authorized one hundred cars and eight new locomotives. Six of these will be built by Baldwin at Philadelphia and delivered via New Orleans by steamboat up the Mississippi and the Ohio. Two were ordered from Anthony Harkness in Cincinnati; the one already delivered is, in neatness of finish, equal to any on the road. $116,052 was earned this year, and a profit of $51,285, even though $30,844 was spent on repairs to the roadbed.

1847. The valley of the Little Miami was visited by a most destructive flood; the water was ten inches higher than for twenty years previously. The partial failure this season in the wheat harvest has prevented the shipment of any considerable quantity of that staple commodity. We have fifteen locomotives in service that ran 160,760 miles during the year, and a sixteenth on the way, "detained in canal"; we carried 78,342 passengers in all and made more than $112,000 net, but most of the profits must go back into improvements and repairs.

1848. There was a great falling off in two of the largest staples of our country, flour and whiskey, because of the dry weather since harvest and the interruption of the river navigation by low water and the diminished price of these articles. 51,468 local passengers and 36,087 through passengers and a vast amount of merchandise have been transported both ways. The fidelity of the agents of the Company has been attested by the fact that no loss of life, and no injury to the person has occurred to our passengers in the course of the year. Rates from Cincinnati to Xenia were $1.90 and to Springfield, 84 miles, $2.50, with a discount of twenty per cent for packages of ten tickets. Earnings were $280,085; and while repairs were greater than ever, net profit was $146,072. The road is now profitable to its shareholders and highly beneficial to the public.

1849. Cholera in its most malignant form prevailed over a great part of Ohio since last summer, especially among the German and Irish immigrants; 4,832, or one in twenty of the population of Cincinnati, died, greater numbers were put to flight and the business of the whole country has been very seriously affected. Nevertheless, along the whole line, villages have sprung up, large bodies of land have been cleared for cultivation, new farms have been enclosed and the log houses of former residents replaced by more substantial buildings. The increase of mills and other manufactories has been very considerable. Cattle-guards are being placed at the ends of all the lanes. Our receipts were up fourteen per cent over last year and our net earnings went to $159,022.

1850. In addition to the regular trains equalling eight per day in one direction, three trains have been engaged in transporting material for the reconstruction of the road. At several points the number of trains passing daily equalled nineteen. Two men returning from the State Fair on an extra train were killed while standing upon the roof of a passenger car by coming in contact with the overhead bracing of Caesar's creek bridge, although the conductor had repeatedly warned the passengers not to get on the tops of the cars. There has been a twenty-five per cent increase in way-freight and forty-five per cent increase in passengers. The Company owns nineteen engines and three more are contracted for; it has twelve 1st class (five with saloons, three 2nd class and four baggage) cars, all in good order. Gross earnings were $465,697. 52,288 through passengers between Cincinnati and Springfield paid over $102,-000 in fares and 92,202 way passengers paid almost exactly the same amount. The principal articles of freight, grain, flour and hogs, brought in $192,000. $90,793 were paid in wages. The net profit was $230,768.

"If the existing connections of our road with other railroads were cut off" said Strader complacently, "the road would be fully sustained . . . from the business of the Little Miami valley, which it drains, and which business, in all human probability, cannot be taken from it, or diminished by competition."

"It will be obvious that the products of the district tributary to our road, have increased even more rapidly than during the three preceding years, and as the country is still new and by no means settled or cultivated in proportion to its capacity, that increase must be progressive for many years."   (VIII)

1851–1860

OPERATIONS AND ALLIANCES

IN the Fifties, the Little Miami, complete, self-contained and prosperous, sought to extend by taking over connecting roads, or by making agreements to interchange traffic and share profits.

THE MANAGEMENT

The management was now made up of men of career, long experienced in constructing and running railroads. The directors, instead of taking a daily part in the business as in the past, were asked only to attend monthly meetings and pass on matters of general policy, or, now and then, to do some special job on an interim committee. Strader and John Kilgour stayed on in charge for a while longer.

WILLIAM H. CLEMENT stepped up, after they left, to first place. Of Huguenot-French descent, like L'Hommedieu, he was born in 1815 at Saratoga Springs, graduated from Rensselaer Polytechnic at Troy, and went to work first as a rodman on the Utica & Schenectady road. 1837 found him in Sandusky, one of the civil engineers for the Mad River.

He came, along with Shoemaker, to the Little Miami in 1838, and took a leading part in building and rebuilding the road, as assistant, chief engineer or as Treasurer and Agent. When the line was finished he was put in charge of operations until 1857, first on the Little Miami and later by the partnership of the Little Miami and the C&X.

During those fourteen years, Clement became almost a legendary figure in American railroad history. Work under him was like the military service; he developed the character of his men by a strict discipline so that they felt, each one in person, the pressure of his reliance on them to discharge their duties properly. Nothing could shake their loyalty to him. During the coal famine in the bitter winter of 1856, when the Little Miami was the only road that ran to the mines and the train crews were called upon to work night and day without rest, they say that not a man left his post.

In 1857 the Ohio & Mississippi asked Clement to be its General Superintendent. The directors of the Little Miami refused permission because of his "long and intimate acquaintance with the details of their business." A month or so later, however, the request was repeated and they let him go, recording "their high appreciation of his talents and long continued and valuable service, which have been so creditable to him and so beneficial to our interests and the general railroad interests of this section of the country, and with their cordial good wishes for his prosperity and happiness in his contemplated field of service."

The Little Miami reclaimed him in December, 1859, electing him president. "We cannot but regard this event," said his predecessor gracefully, "as a most favorable omen." And indeed, he kept the ser-

vice at its highest pitch throughout the strenuous days of the Civil War.

ERASMUS GEST was the son of Joseph, first city surveyor of Cincinnati. After his father went blind, he finished laying out the plan of the city with the measuring rod which was two per cent longer than U. S. standard, and which has been such a bother to surveyors and conveyancers ever since. That done, he went from one engineering job to the next —among others, to the Whitewater canal out of Cincinnati, to a canal in Maryland at Havre de Grace, and to the Ohio & Mississippi, as successor to Ormsby Mitchell. He came to the Little Miami in 1848, helped locate the line of the C&X and became its Chief Engineer. Later he was president of the O&M and went from there with the Cincinnati, Wilmington & Zanesvile. He built and operated street railways in Cincinnati, and died a rich old bachelor in 1908.

Gest was an able mathematician, a notable engineer, and a hard-headed, driving executive. The people in the Over-the-Rhine district of Cincinnati still remember him: for when they blocked his carline, he said: "The Dutch are hell." He always finished whatever job was before him, and he was never afraid to swim upstream.

DIRECTORS begin to appear with names honored more for other activities than for railroading. For instance:

Alphonso Taft; Vermonter, Yale graduate, eminent lawyer, Judge of the Superior Court, Secretary of War, Attorney General and Ambassador of the United States, whose mantle fell on his distinguished son, William Howard Taft.

Reuben R. Springer; Kentuckian, steamboat clerk, son-in-law and partner of John Kilgour, patron of music and benefactor of Cincinnati.

Nathaniel Wright; a long-time director and for one year President, learned in the law, and respected by everyone.

CONSTRUCTION

In the floodtide of railroad building during the early Fifties, the directors planned to double-track the Little Miami from end to end. It was done by fits and starts, going ahead when money was easy, and slowing down when bonds were hard to sell, but it never went beyond the junction at Morrow with the CW&Z. The mileage of the Little Miami and of the C&X in 1856, when they united, was almost what it is today.

Little Miami	Main Track ..	83½ miles
	Double Track	20¼ miles
	Side Track ..	12½ miles
		116¼ miles
C&X	Main Track ..	54½ miles
	Side Track ..	8¾ miles
		63¼ miles

In 1853, all of the old flat bar rail had been taken up, and the line relaid with T-rail. The newly-invented Bessemer process made steel plentiful and cheap.

"Our road," said Strader in 1856, "is inferior to no road in smoothness, solidity and capacity to admit the safe and rapid transport of heavy travel." (1st J.)

DEPOTS and better facilities at the terminals grew in importance as shippers began sending their goods over other lines, and the competition for passengers and freight stiffened.

The little old passenger shed at Cincinnati, in use since 1844, was wholly unfitted for the needs of the business and something better was required for the main railroad entrance to the city. The Little Miami secured extensive grounds, "extending from the paved streets of the city to the Ohio river, including an excellent landing, and within a short distance of the public wharves now frequented by steamboats." A passenger house, 450 by 80 feet, "an elegant and convenient structure, reflecting a great credit to William McCammon, under whose superintendence it was designed and erected" (XI), was completed and brought into use in 1853.

At the other end of the line, the Columbus & Xenia, with the concurrence of the Little Miami, joined the Cleveland, Columbus & Cincinnati Railroad to build a union passenger depot in the heart of Columbus.

FINANCE

All of the ten-year unsecured obligations which had been issued in the Forties were paid in full between 1850 and 1860. The early months of 1853, when the Bank of England discount rate fell to two per cent, seemed a God-given time to secure any money that might be needed in the future. A million and a half of thirty-year six per cent non-convertible bonds, secured by mortgage to James F. D. Lanier of New York, were authorized. On the day appointed for the public offering in New York, a sudden stringency in the money market occurred and "owing to the extreme scarcity of money and the impossibility of selling even the best of securities" they were temporarily withdrawn, to be sold in later years when times were easier.

Outstanding stock increased almost to the $3,000,000 authorized by law, principally because of the constant conversion of short-term bonds. From 1852 on, dividends were paid regularly in cash, or occasionally in bonds, when money was scarce. A certificate for $92.50, issued in December, 1855, in payment of Dividend No. 19, went astray and was brought in seventy-five years later by a bartender who had traded the finder out of it for a drink of whiskey.

Assets, representing principally construction of the road, depots and machinery, and, in some part, investments in other roads over which the Little Miami wanted a say, also increased in proportion.

For the figures, see the tables.

CONNECTIONS AND TRAFFIC

The liaisons and rivalries of the Ohio railroads from 1851 to 1860 are so profuse and so bewildering that

STATISTICS, 1851–1861

Year	Bonds		Capital Stock		Assets
		Payments	Total Issued	Dividends	
Dec. 1850	Outstanding: Eastern Loan of 1845 . $ 190,000 1846 Loan .... $ 61,000 1848 Loan .... $ 200,000 1850 Loan .... $ 165,000 Total .... $ 710,000		$1,418,875		$2,729,375 $232,608 in C&X stock $ 1,200 in Cinti & Sandusky Telegraph
1851	New Issues 1848 Bonds .... $ 81,000 Income Bonds of 1851 . $ 298,000 Cincinnati depot site purchased with stock.	$ 7,000 $100,000 ——————— $107,000	$1,627,096	Stock: 10%	$3,285,760 $4,871 more in C&X stock
1852	None issued Great conversion of short-term bonds into stock this year.	$ 5,000 $143,000 $ 51,000 $146,000 ——————— $345,000	$2,370,787	Cash: 10%	$3,684,564 $124,571 more in C&X stock $ 11,716 in Cincinnati & Hillsboro stock

Year	Bonds		Capital Stock		Assets
	New Issues	Payments	Total Issued	Dividends	
1853	6% Mortgage Bonds of 1853 .... $138,000 1850 Loan paid in full. Bad times, 1853 bonds peddled about locally.	$144,000 $ 14,000 $158,000	$2,668,402	Cash: 10%	$4,373,823 $167,921 more in C&X stock $150,000 in Springfield, Mt. Vernon & Pittsburgh $32,630 in Lake Steamboat line
1854	Bonds of 1853 .... $ 246,000	$ 17,000 $142,000 $159,000	$2,963,921	Cash: 5%	$4,473,903 $31,116 more in C&X stock $50,150 more in SMtV&P stock
1855	Bonds of 1853 .... $ 141,000 Last of Eastern Loan of 1845 paid in full. Floating debt reduced.	$ 17,000 $ 3,000 $ 20,000	$2,981,327	Bonds: 10%	$4,598,680 $14,734 more in C&X stock
1856	Bonds of 1853 .... $ 295,000 1846 Loan paid in full. Balance of floating debt funded.	$ 61,000	$2,981,282	Bonds: 5%	$4,819,180 C&X investment reduced $25,600

Year	Bonds		Capital Stock		Assets
	New Issues	Payments	Total Issued	Dividends	
1857	Bonds of 1853 .... $ 161,000		$2,981,293	Cash: 5% Bonds: 5%	$4,571,580 Cincinnati & Hillsboro investment reduced $2,454 SMtV&P investment reduced $196,150
	Panic and deep, long-lasting depression.				
1858	$ 311,000	$138,000	$2,981,293	Cash: 9%	$4,709,137
1859	Bonds of 1853 .... $10,000		$2,981,293	Cash: 12%	$4,763,694
Dec. 1860	Outstanding: Cincinnati Loan .... $ 100,000 Income Bonds of 1851 $ 7,000 Mortgage Bonds of 1853 $1,300,000 Total $1,407,000		$2,981,270	Cash: 8%	$4,852,007 Including: C&X .... $425,650 H&C .... $ 9,262 SMtV&P .... $ 4,000 Sundry stocks .... $ 3,090

they can hardly be understood unless the story of them is told in chronological order, sometimes almost from week to week. And all the little railroads, scrambling over each other to make friends, and every one struggling to get ahead of the rest, seem so human in their hopes and fears that the telling falls almost of its own accord into a sort of dramatic dialogue.

THE CAST OF CHARACTERS

The Narrator; who tries to explain what is going on and fills in the gaps.

The Hero and His Friends

The Little Miami; now called "Old Reliable" everywhere; short in stature but strong in resources, credit and standing.

The Columbus & Xenia (the C&X); a ward of The Little Miami and tied to it in an "indissoluble bond."

The Dayton, Xenia & Belpre (the DX&B); a small upstart; soon gobbled up by The Little Miami and the C&X.

The Dayton & Western (the D&W); a tributary and feeder of western traffic.

The Cincinnati & Hillsboro (the C&H); which vanished into the insides of the Marietta & Cincinnati.

The Marietta & Cincinnati (the M&C); first known as the *Belpre & Cincinnati,* it eventually became part of the main line of the B&O.

The Cincinnati, Wilmington & Zanesville (the CW&Z); taken over by the Pennsylvania.

OPERATIONS AND ALLIANCES

The Mad River & Lake Erie; the earliest friend, but always feeble and distressful.

The Springfield, Mt. Vernon & Pittsburgh (the SMtV&P); a pawn eventually captured by the other side.

Allies at Columbus

The Cleveland, Columbus & Cincinnati (the CC&C); intimate and staunch friend of the Little Miami; ending as part of the Big Four and the New York Central System.

The Central Ohio; extending the B&O west from Wheeling to Columbus.

The Steubenville & Indiana (the S&I); protegé of the Pennsylvania and later part of the PC&StL.

The Pittsburgh & Steubenville (the P&S); extension of the Pennsylvania from Pittsburgh, the S&I to Pittsburgh; also consolidated in the PC&StL.

The Westerners

The Ohio & Mississippi (the O&M); a sprawling sort of fellow, six feet wide.

The Indiana Central; Hoosier partner of the D&W at Richmond.

The Indianapolis & Cincinnati (the I&C); just another Hoosier.

The Southerners

The Central Kentucky; headed from Covington for the deep South, but stopped inert at the foot of the Cumberland plateau.

The Louisville & Nashville (the L&N); cause of frustration to Cincinnati.

The Northern Routes

The Lake Shore; a combination of the following roads, and eventually the main line of the New York Central system:

The Cleveland, Painesville & Ashtabula; the dominant factor;

The Cleveland & Toledo; a combination of *The Junction Road* and others;

The Northern Indiana; Toledo westwardly to the Ohio line.

The Pittsburgh, Ft. Wayne & Chicago (the PFtW&C); part of the Pennsylvania system, formed in 1868, out of:

The Ohio & Pennsylvania (the O&P); from Crestline on CC&C to Pittsburgh;

The Ohio & Indiana; Crestline to Ft. Wayne; *The Ft. Wayne & Chicago.*

The Bellefontaine & Indiana; familiarly known as the *Bee Line.*

The Atlantic & Great Western (the A&GW); connecting link between the broad gauge Erie and the broad gauge O&M.

The Eastern Systems

The Pennsylvania; it reached Pittsburgh in 1852.

The Baltimore & Ohio (the B&O); on January 1, 1853, the first train ran into Wheeling, and in 1857 the first train, by way of the *Northwestern Virginia* branch, ran into Parkersburg.

The Erie; the Calamity Jane of railroads, ravished again and again but always coming up for more.

The New York Central (the NYC); ten separate

strips, end to end, from Buffalo to Albany, not made one until 1869.

The Southern; King Cotton's royal highway, from Charleston and Savannah into the hinterland.

The Villain and His Gang

The Cincinnati, Hamilton & Dayton (the CH&D); here caused to seem unprincipled and sinister, but in reality only trying, with might and main, to make a living.

The Dayton & Michigan (the D&M); operated by the CH&D as if its own.

The Eaton & Hamilton (the E&H); rival of the D&W.

Others

The Cincinnati, Lebanon & Northern, the *Cincinnati & Dayton,* etc.; creatures of the Lebanonites.

Presidents of Railroads, Bankers, Eye-witnesses, etc., etc., as needed.

THE SCENE

The curtain rises on the broad plains of Ohio, fringed to the south and southeast by the river bluffs along the great valley, and by the ragged skyline of the Alleghanies on the east. Westerly are level prairies and woodland, unbroken beyond eyesight except for the silvery line of the Mississippi. The backdrop is Lake Erie, blue and sparkling in summer or glittering with ice six months of the year.

The lighting is brilliant, except for a stormy moment in 1854 and during the panic of 1857. The tempo is always headlong and violent. Throughout the play, behind the leading actors, thousands of Irish and the Dutch are furiously digging roadbeds and laying rails.

An' it's work all day, with no sugar in yer tay,
And dhr-r-rill, ye tarriers, dhr-r-rill!

Locomotives belching wood-sparks run to and fro; sternwheelers glide in flocks on the river; and upstage, boats pass and repass along the shores of the lake.

THE PROLOGUE

The Narrator. During the next ten years, new railroads will be born at the rate of one each and every twenty-four hours. The two hundred and sixty millions of gold from California and such profits of good business as do not find employment elsewhere are ready at hand to extend the rails into vacant spaces. Today in 1850, there are 8,590 miles of track in the United States, 1,200 miles will be laid each year, so that when the curtain falls in 1860 there will be 30,794 miles, costing an average of $35,000 per mile, or over a billion dollars. Right here on these plains before you, where the thoroughfares of commerce converge, almost three thousand miles, paralleling and intersecting each other, will be built, and will be paid for, half from stock bought by local subscribers and half with bonds sold to bankers in the East and in Europe. You will wonder at the insane energy and the pouring out of money.

Down here at the footlights you see Cincinnati, its cheerful red-brick houses, the graceful stone spire of its Georgian Cathedral, and its Burnet House, be-

PUBLIC LANDING, CINCINNATI.
(*Note:* The *Jacob Strader* is heading downstream for Louisville.)

lieved to be the most spacious and probably the best hotel in all the world. It will grow twelve per cent in population each year—more rapidly than any city in America—from 116,110 at this day to a quarter of a million in the next ten years. Another quarter of a million live between the two Miami rivers. Cincinnati is second in the country in manufacturing clothing with 248 factories, and iron with sixty foundries and ten rolling mills. It makes and deals in more than a hundred and fifty tons of foodstuffs every year. They call it "Porkopolis." It dominates trade with the South.

Eight hundred flat-bottomed steamboats, three or four times as many as on the Great Lakes, from fast passenger-packets down to cargo boats, ply the endless waterways. A hundred and eight million tons of freight will pass in 1851 down the river and through New Orleans. This is the gilded era of the great floating palaces, of the pilots, the roustabouts and the gamblers.

Some people claim that the railroads will in time displace the river trade. But how can that ever happen until the trains are equipped to carry loads of the size the boats can handle? And just suppose the railroad does win out in the end, Cincinnati already has six hundred and thirty-nine miles, five hundred and eighty-six are in progress and over a thousand are undertaken; if the railroad must settle the destiny of the cities struggling for supreme ascendancy, "fourteen great trunk roads will radiate to every point of the compass, each one terminating at a great commercial point on the Seaboard, or in a mineral or agricultural region, with all their influences converging to this centre." Cincinnati will always continue to be the gateway of commerce between the North and the South, from the Alleghanies to the Mississippi.

1851

The Little Miami. (To the world in general) " We take pleasure in calling your attention . . . to the very great improvement which has taken place in the facilities and comforts extended to passengers. . . . There has been a perceptible improvement in hotels, steamboats, and passenger trains, and in the attention paid, generally, to the comfort and safety of travelers. . . . The trip, either by Buffalo or Dunkirk, to the Eastern commercial cities, is accomplished with a degree of speed and comfort heretofore unknown, and with scarcely any danger or fatigue; while, for those who journey for health or pleasure, our connections with the great Northern Lakes, and with the fine railroad and steamboat lines leading to Niagara, Saratoga, Newport, Montreal, Quebec, and other places of resort, give to our Road great advantages. . . . The alternation of land and water conveyances, with the advantage of resting at night on board of comfortable steamboats, give to this route great attractiveness, and cause it to be thronged with passengers." (IX)

> *Singing through the forests,*
> *Rattling over ridges,*
> *Shooting under arches,*
> *Rumbling over bridges,*

OPERATIONS AND ALLIANCES 97

Whizzing through the mountains,
Buzzing o'er the vale,
Bless me this is pleasant,
RIDING ON THE RAIL!

The Little Miami. (To the Cleveland, Columbus & Cincinnati) Our morning express starts from Cincinnati at 5:20 for Xenia and will meet you via the C&X in Columbus at 11:30.

The CC&C. We'll get the passengers to Cleveland by suppertime. A steamboat of the first class, either the *Empire State* or the *Buckeye State,* will be waiting there to ferry them overnight to Buffalo. They catch the morning express to Albany, and the evening boat down the Hudson to New York. The trains may be delayed awaiting the arrival of steamboats detained by rough waters or by imperfect connection of trains still further eastward. It is difficult to produce entire harmony of action and exact punctuality in so long a line of travel.

The Little Miami. (To the Mad River, but a little less cordially) Our afternoon express leaves Cincinnati at 2:30. You are to take over at Springfield and arrive at Sandusky at 6:00 the next morning.

The Mad River. The regular day boats from Sandusky dock at Dunkirk in time to catch the night train over the Erie. Our fare is only eight-eighty to Buffalo—the CC&C charges ten dollars, you know.

The Narrator. (Sweeping the stage with a glance) Look, the Dayton & Western has wheedled $50,000 from Dayton, sold $309,000 of stock and $300,000 in ten-year bonds, and gone frantically to work. It hopes to connect somewhere on the Ohio-Indiana boundary with the Bee Line for Indianapolis. Up in the north, the Ohio & Pennsylvania and the Ohio & Indiana are building east and west from the CC&C at Crestline. The Ohio law forces them to adopt the four-foot-ten-inch gauge and that excess inch and a half will give the Pennsylvania a lot of trouble later on. Further south, the Central Ohio has borrowed an engineer from the B&O and is on the way from Zanesville toward Newark and Columbus.

Out in the west, way off stage, Illinois has granted a charter to the Ohio & Mississippi at last. Erasmus Gest, called in to check Ormsby Mitchell's survey, estimates the cost of the line at about ten millions, but this is decried as extravagant. Contracts for grading have been let, and people along the line subscribe a million dollars.

Across the river from Cincinnati the Covington & Lexington has started toward the South, and far away, beyond the Cumberland plateau, the great Southern system has long since reached Knoxville and more recently Chattanooga.

Over on the eastern side of the Alleghanies, the Eastern trunklines, like eager young giants, are peering through the passes, or stretching around the upper end where the foothills dwindle off into lake terraces. The Pennsylvania builds from the western end of the Portage toward Pittsburgh. The Baltimore & Ohio with 5,000 men and 1,250 horses is forcing its way for seventy miles through the boldest mountain regions east of the Mississippi. The Erie has at last completed, at a cost of more than twenty millions, 445 miles of bad track from Piermont-on-Hudson to Dunkirk. There Millard Fillmore, President of the United States, Daniel Webster and William H. Seward come in April to celebrate the opening of the line from the ocean to the lakes.

The Ohio legislature is in session and deputations of small-town celebrities are milling about in Columbus. That crowd is asking a charter for a line to connect Springfield with the CC&C at Loudenville, up-state and so on to Pittsburgh. The next one, even more ambitious, under the grandiose name of the Atlantic & Great Western, wants to run from Warren up in the northeast corner southwestwardly 246 miles to Dayton and beyond that to the state line to pick up traffic from the southwest. The Cincinnati, Wilmington & Zanesville is incorporated for three millions, and its backers dash off to extort $775,000 in subscriptions from the towns and counties through which it will pass. The Belpre & Cincinnati asks authority to build from the bank of the Ohio river opposite Parkersburg clear to Cincinnati, but a gang of hard-bitten New Englanders from the Ohio Purchase rush in with $350,000 in subscriptions, snatch the charter away and persuade the legislature to change the name to "The Marietta & Cincinnati."

The M&C. (With the boldness of extreme youth) Archibald Kennedy, who built the Vermont Central, has located our line; it has no grades of more than fifty feet to the mile from Chillicothe east to Athens or west as far as Hillsborough. We have $1,144,000 in sight from government bodies. Once we get to Marietta we can take our choice and either go upriver to Wheeling and make the B&O bid against the Hempfield Road that belongs to the Pennsylvania for our business, or else we can run a short branch down to meet the Northwestern Virginia that the B&O talks of building to Parkersburg. Our road runs through inexhaustible deposits of iron and coal, and it's 120 miles shorter from Marietta to Cincinnati than by steamboat on the Ohio river. It is our manifest destiny to be the *Great Central American Railway*.

(The M&C spies the Little Miami transporting material from its line at Loveland to build the Hillsborough & Cincinnati toward Chillicothe and perhaps further.)

The M&C. (Calling to the H&C) Hey you, you over there. How about taking over your line from Hillsborough to Loveland?

The H&C. (Looking to the Little Miami for courage) Not so fast. The Little Miami is going to operate our road for us; it's surveyed all the way to Jackson, and we aim to parallel you all the way across the state.

The M&C. (Taken aback, but still putting up a front) All right. But you better look out. We've surveyed a much better route than yours through Greenfield.

(The Little Miami sums at the end of the year.)

The Little Miami. The harvests have been abundant and business is just beginning to come in from our connections. Our passenger cars are of the most modern construction; new trucks with lateral motion

OPERATIONS AND ALLIANCES 101

and India Rubber Springs have been substituted for the old trucks; and Turner's Patent Brake Connection has been applied to all cars, and adds greatly to the safety of passengers. We keep twenty-five locomotives busy, from the *Xenia* of thirteen and a half tons to the *Atlas* of twenty-three tons. 174,089 passengers went over the road, and we have 230 freight cars in service. Transportation receipts for passengers, freight and rail were $487,815, net profits $297,457.

1852

The Little Miami. (Cordially to the CC&C) Our passengers are getting off at Xenia to take the next train to Columbus instead of going through Springfield. Now how about a consolidation? Suppose we appoint committees and see what can be done.

The CC&C. If you will bring in the C&X, we can get the Cleveland, Painesville and Ashtabula to join us. When the other roads along the lake shore into Buffalo are completed this spring, we'll give uninterrupted railway communication from Cincinnati to New York.

The Little Miami. In the meantime, let's run our lines together and agree not to make conflicting arrangements with any other road. One superintendent can manage the southern division from Columbus to Cincinnati and another the northern division up to Cleveland, with a joint committee to supervise the whole thing.

The CC&C. That steamboat line of ours to Buffalo is in trouble, and wants us to carry their maintenance charges while they are fighting the Mad River steamers.

The Little Miami. All right, we'll share with you up to $35,000. Our intercourse has always been entirely harmonious and satisfactory, and is conducive to mutual prosperity and to the convenience of the public.

The Mad River. (Off by itself) How in thunder are we going to get along? Here we've already spent two millions, three hundred and fifty thousand on our road, and now we have to increase our capital stock to six millions. We can't force an unwilling connection on the Little Miami, and we can't fight the eastern lines trending to the Mississippi valley. Our receipts are cut in half during the winter months when the lake-boats are tied up by ice. We must secure an entrance to Cincinnati and get a through connection to the East somehow, or we'll never be anything except a local freight road.

The CH&D. (Aside) Our capital stock is up to two and a half millions already. We had to furnish the Hamilton & Eaton with $100,000 in engines and cars. The Dayton & Michigan won't ever get to Toledo unless we lend them credit. Some day, we hope to complete an immense system of intercommunication in an agricultural region of vast extent and unrivaled productiveness. But we can't wait forever. Right now The Miami & Erie canal is dividing the local freight to Dayton with us. We'll never be able to survive unless we get an outlet to the East.

The Mad River. (Aloud to the CH&D) See here,

you and we are natural allies. We are pressing the extension of our line from Springfield to Dayton. Why can't we arrange with you to exchange Cincinnati business?

The CH&D. Nothing would suit us better. And what's more, we'll contribute a hundred thousand if you'll give us a share in your line of propellers from Sandusky to Buffalo.

(A delegation from Lebanon sidles up to the CH&D.)

The Spokesman. The Little Miami has broken every promise it has made to build us a branch to Lebanon. We are organizing our own road, the Cincinnati, Lebanon & Xenia. But it's hard to raise money since this new Ohio constitution has stopped subscribing for stock by the towns and counties. We're trying to negotiate a construction contract at twenty-five thousand dollars a mile, one-fourth in cash, one-fourth in stock, and half in bonds.

The CH&D. You're welcome if you want to join our line at Carthage and run into Cincinnati over our tracks.

The Little Miami. (Breaks in) Our engineer, Clement, has just called our attention to the propriety of placing a second track through Lebanon under contract. We'll need some of you Lebanon people to help us get options for rights of way.

(The delegation immediately splits into two factions. They go out cursing each other.)

(The Pennsylvania suddenly breaks through to Pittsburgh, the first of the young giants to reach the Ohio river.)

The Pennsylvania. (Speaking by J. Edgar Thomson, its engineer in construction days and now its president; young, forceful and domineering) The Management of the Pennsylvania begs to report with great pleasure that a single track railroad has been opened to trade and travel between Philadelphia and Pittsburgh. We have sold $3,000,000 above par out of our new five million bond issue, and we are starting to build our Mountain Division around the Portage. The Hempfield road running from our main line at Greenburg to Wheeling is in progress.

The Little Miami. (To its stockholders) "A favorable season for business, and a highly prosperous condition of the country, have fairly tested the capacity of our road, by throwing on it a large amount of business, which has been transacted with facility and promptness, and in a manner, as we have reason to believe, in every way satisfactory to the public. . . . Nearly three thousand head of horses and cattle, on their way to New York, have passed over our road, instead of being driven over the mountains. . . . More than 5,000 hogsheads of tobacco have gone to the Atlantic cities over our road, instead of seeking a market in New Orleans." (X) Way passengers and through passengers were both over 100,000. We earned $526,746 and paid a ten per cent dividend in cash.

1853

The Narrator. The Baltimore & Ohio, second of the young giants, escapes from the mountains at Wheeling. "Through every vicissitude of climate,

OPERATIONS AND ALLIANCES 105

obstructed by interminable rocks, opposed by a succession of barriers altogether without a parallel in the progress of similar enterprises, by day and night it has pressed forward." New Year's day is celebrated in the bustling little river town by 500 guests who arrive on the first train. They cross the suspension bridge newly built by Roebling, and gaze down the National Road that runs due west hundreds of miles to the Mississippi.

In these bright unclouded days, the railroads, one after another, are opened to travel in Ohio. Locomotives begin to displace the track-workers. The Ohio & Pennsylvania is in operation from Crestline where it takes the Little Miami and CC&C passengers to Pittsburgh, and the Central Ohio is finished from Zanesville to Columbus. The little roads, the CW&Z, the D&W, the I&C at Lawrenceburg twenty miles down the Ohio from Cincinnati, the Central Kentucky across the river and all the others, run trains as far as their tracks are laid. Dirt is flying along the line of the Steubenville & Indiana and on the Pittsburgh & Steubenville beyond the Ohio boundary, both of them backed by the Pennsylvania.

Work on the Ohio & Mississippi was stopped last year by cholera in the construction camps. That restless man, Ormsby Mitchell, has crossed the ocean to London and excited the admiration and envy of the financial world by raising $2,750,000 in three months. The O&M is going ahead at last.

(The Little Miami and the C&X stand together, looking over the scene.)

The Little Miami. "Our line . . . from Cincinnati to Columbus, although constructed and owned by separate corporations, forms naturally but one road; the greater and more valuable part of the business passing from either extremity of the line extends to the other, and the interests of our respective stockholders are the same. It is obviously convenient, as well as economical, that the two roads should be operated by one set of officers, and by machinery held and worked in common." (1st J.)

The C&X. Why don't we unite permanently? The public will be as well served, and agents will be fewer, expenses less, and the responsibility better concentrated.

The Little Miami. For better, for worse, we two shall never part. We'll put our gross earnings into a joint account to pay current expense, and distribute the residue, after reserves to keep the properties in good repair, in dividends at the same rate on both stocks. The companies will remain intact and distinct, of course, each with its own officers and separate properties. Any new equipment we may have to buy will be held in common in proportion to our capital, one-third to you, two-thirds to us.

(They sign the Contract of Union of November 30,
    1853. To them comes The Springfield,
        Mt. Vernon & Pittsburgh.)

The SM&V&P. We need $200,000 more to get to Delaware. If you subscribe, we'll use our road exclusively for travel to Cincinnati and not ticket over any other road.

The Little Miami. (Aside to the C&X) If *we* don't help, the CH&D will grab it. (To the SMtV&P) All right, we'll pay you $150,000 in our 1853 bonds right now on your stock, bill our business through Springfield over your road, and divide fares in proportion to the length of our lines. But don't say a word to anybody about it.

The CH&D. (Lurking near and overhearing, aside) There's our chance. (Runs over to the CC&C) Did you know that the Little Miami is going to short-cut your line and ship to Springfield and over the SMtV&P instead of through Columbus? That's the kind of partner you've got. We can offer you something better. The Mad River has remodelled its road and replaced all the old flat bar with T-rail. We run the smoothest, freest of dust, pleasantest and best-built line in Ohio, and it's forty miles shorter from the lake to the Ohio river and twenty-two miles nearer Indianapolis than any other. The Junction Road between Sandusky and Cleveland will be done in a month or so. The Hamilton & Eaton has the Dayton & Western licked and is picking up a lot of business from Indiana. We are working on a road from Hamilton direct to Indianapolis. We carry over twelve hundred passengers every day. Now, why don't the two of us get together? Even if you insist on sticking to the Little Miami, there's no point in trying to cripple each other.

The CC&C. (Cautiously) We'll talk it over with the Little Miami. (Whispers to the Little Miami) It looks as if they had something worth while there. They can't help but get some traffic and whatever they steal from us might be permanently diverted. What do you think?

The Little Miami. (Trying hard to be fair, aloud to the CC&C and the CH&D together) "The vast population and rich products of the Great Miami valley must always afford a local business more than sufficient to give profitable employment to a railroad; and that valley is so separated, geographically, from the valley of the Little Miami, that the resources of each are naturally drained by its own road, and neither can be diverted from its natural channel. Of the passenger and through business, there are portions which fall naturally to each road, and there will remain other portions which might be transacted with equal advantage by either company, but, to obtain which, neither could be justifiable in making any ruinous sacrifice, as it is a share which either can well afford to yield, and which, therefore, both should be satisfied to share as circumstances may direct." (XI)

The CH&D. (Pleased and oily) Well then, how about an alliance of the Little Miami, the C&X and the CC&C as the Eastern line, and of the CH&D, the Mad River and the Junction Road as the Western line, with a general ticket office for both in Cincinnati? You take sixty per cent of the earnings—forty per cent will be enough to satisfy our crowd.

The Little Miami and *The CC&C.* Agreed. We'll try it for a while.

(The Cincinnati & Hillsborough and the Marietta & Cincinnati, scowling at each other, get the Little Miami in between them)

The C&H. (In one ear) We've spent half a million on our road, and we threw four thousand hogs and farm products in large amounts onto your line last year. We run three trains a day, and we simply can't carry all the freight offered us. Business will increase when we reach the coal region in Jackson County next year. The B&O doesn't trust the Marietta and wants us to go on to Parkersburg and meet the Northwestern Virginia projecting down from their main line at Grafton.

The M&C. (In the other ear) You better not fool around with the C&H. We already have thirty-three miles contracted and 1,200 men, three hundred horses and two of those new steam-shovels on the job. We've just sold a lot of bonds in France and have plenty of money. We penetrate the best part of the fertile valley of the Scioto and we'll pay a nice price for the use of your track from Loveland to Cincinnati and of your grounds there.

The Little Miami. (Looking straight ahead) "It would not become us, offering, as we do, connections with either or both . . . to make any remark as to their comparative advantages or their prospects. Both roads traverse highly productive districts and will be valuable adjuncts to the trade of Cincinnati. Our depot arrangements . . . will be of the most liberal character, and will afford convenient accommodation for any aggregate of business, however large, that may be concentrated there." (X)

The M&C. (Aside, in fear and doubt) We'll have to kill the H&C or else it will kill us. The Pennsylvania has bought a lot of our stock and that means we'll be forced to build up to Wheeling. Our best outlet, all the same, is over the B&O, but we have never summoned the temerity to ask them for a dollar.

The Little Miami. (Cogitating, well pleased about the year's work) "There have been on alternations of activity and rest in our operations. Throughout the year, and within each month of the year, our force has been fully and profitably employed, and been gradually increased and renewed to meet the accruing demands of the business. . . . Our track traverses a productive soil, inhabited by an industrious people, and it connects a large city with a number of thriving towns, as well as with a prosperous agricultural population. . . . There is no barren land in the vicinity of our road—scarcely an acre which may not be made to yield a valuable return for the labor bestowed on it. . . . It cannot be doubted that the whole Little Miami valley, and the rich plains beyond it, will, before many years shall elapse, be thickly settled with farms, manufactories, and country residences." (XI) Since the Contract of Union with the C&X, we are working thirty-nine locomotives that ran 505,387 miles during the year, 30 first-class passenger cars and 10 second-class, 445 freight cars of all kinds, and 26 hand-cars for the section hands. One passenger attempting to get off the train while in motion was drawn under the wheels of the last car; a second committed suicide by throwing himself under a train running at high speed, while he was laboring under delirium, caused by intemperance; and a third fell from the platform while the cars were being shifted, but he was in a state of intoxication at the time. Earnings increased $140,812 over last year to about $670,000, and net earnings to $352,132.

1854

The Narrator. The Pennsylvania trains are still being hauled by horses from the Broad Street station to the outskirts of Philadelphia, but it has completed its Mountain Division around the Portage, over and through the Alleghanies. It is lending $300,000 to the Ohio & Pennsylvania for its bridge over the river into Pittsburgh, and $300,000 more to the Ohio & Indiana to finish the road as far as Ft. Wayne.

Only one break remains in the entire trip from Chicago to Buffalo. At Erie, Pennsylvania, gangs of the native brigands still transfer passengers and freight from one station to the other with the utmost of profit to themselves and of annoyance to everyone else. When the railroads try to cross the gap, a mob, led by the Mayor of the town, tears up the rail as fast as it is laid, so that at last the militia has to be called out.

(Enter the C&H and the M&W, hand in hand.)

The C&H. (To the Little Miami) We're sorry, but we must cancel our contract with you. The M&C has taken a perpetual lease of our line. Our first sixteen miles out of Loveland will be their main line and the rest of it to Hillsboro will be just a feeder.

The M&C. Of course, we still want your track to Cincinnati, for a while at least. You are crowded with your own business and some day perhaps we may build our own line.

The Little Miami. We have graded a second track to Loveland and thence to Morrow. "It is due to the public and to the roads connecting with ours and is imperatively required by a proper regard for the safety of passengers." (XII) We have ordered all our trains to approach Loveland with great care; the engineer retaining perfect control and being sure the way is clear before passing the junction.

(At Morrow, further up the line of the Little Miami, the Cincinnati, Wilmington & Zanesville speaks.)

The CW&Z. We are heading up Todd's Fork from Morrow, with four bridges in the space of a couple of miles but with little curvature and light grading, toward the finest agricultural district in Ohio. Soon we'll be at Lancaster, a hundred and twenty-five miles from Cincinnati. There we get coal down the canal from the rich Hocking valley fields, reload and lay it down in Cincinnati for sixteen cents a bushel. As soon as it can be put on cars at the mines, it won't cost more than twelve cents and still afford a fair price to the railroad for transportation.

(The cocky little figure of the Dayton, Xenia & Belpre pops up at Xenia.)

The DX&B. (In a piping voice) Here *we* are, eighteen miles from Dayton, ready to give speedy means of transit to all east and west travel from Columbus and Zanesville to Dayton and Indianapolis. As soon as we sell a million and a half of stock and a half million of bonds, we'll push on to Rattlesnake Creek, and then to Belpre and settle the hash of that Marietta crowd.

The D&W. (From behind the DX&B) *We* have made a twenty-year arrangement with the Central Indiana to exchange business to and from Indianapolis.

The Narrator. See how the thunderheads have spread and the skies are suddenly overcast. In August of 1854 the excesses of prosperity brought on a stock-market crisis. Men suddenly stopped to look around and wonder why all the hurry. Too many railroad securities have been issued and the public has lost all faith for the time being. It is a bad moment. As business falls off, tempers shorten and competitors grow more bitter than ever.

The Little Miami. (To the CH&D) The Lake Shore people say you put up a dirty fight against their lake steamers last summer with your *Mississippi* and your *St. Louis* from Sandusky, and that now you are trying to blackmail them with your Junction Road into Cleveland. They tell us they refuse to honor your tickets over their lines any longer. So unless you and the Mad River withdraw your boats, we can't sell any more tickets over the Lake Shore for you at the Cincinnati office.

The CH&D. (In a fury) You want us to quit, —never! It's nothing but usurpation of authority to throw us out of your ticket-office, and an abandonment and desertion of duty. The Lake Shore is trying to hamper, harass and injure its neighbors in Ohio, and is determined to create a monopoly of travel to the East. But nobody is going to shut us out of our fair proportion. We'll reduce our passenger fares from Cincinnati to the Lake to two dollars and seventy-five cents and take freight at two eighty per ton. We'll show you how to get business.

The Little Miami. (Indignantly) We can bring our fares down too, below the remunerating point, and those who might prefer to travel over our road shall have a daily opportunity of doing so at the same price you charge. "The employment of runners, solicitors and other means of puffing particular lines of travel, and enticing passengers, by which travelers are greatly annoyed, and often grossly misled, are both expensive and discreditable to those who employ them and should be universally discountenanced. . . . It has been our practice, heretofore, in all our intercourse with other companies, to unite with a strict good faith, a conciliatory spirit. . . . It is alike incumbent upon us all to fulfill our engagements to each other, and to the public; and this cannot well be done without concert and harmony of action, to secure which it is necessary not only that each company perform its own work satisfactorily, but that it be satisfied with its legitimate share of the aggregate gain. . . . All that we have to regret in this matter is the temporary interruption of certain rules of courtesy and fairness, which we had observed, and supposed to have been generally consented to, and the consequent breach of harmony between our road and others with whom we desired no other than the most friendly relations." (XII)

The Little Miami. (To itself at the end of the

year) "A natural consequence of the dry weather which prevailed during the summer and fall, has been the universal prevalence of low water, and the interruption of navigation. The immediate effect of this would be to throw upon the railroads the freight and passengers, of which a large proportion would otherwise pass by the navigable streams; but experience has shown that the general effect of this state of things is disastrous to railroads, as well as other interests. . . . Nearly all the immense supplies of coal, iron and lumber and a portion of the flour of the Western States, are produced in localities where water is required for their transport. . . . Railroads and water navigation are both necessary, and must exist as cooperative influences, or as feeders to each other."

(XII) Our road has continued to receive, and we hope to merit, a full share of public favor. The traveling public demands better accommodations and greater security from accident. The speed of our trains has increased from sixteen miles per hour, which was considered almost hazardous a few years since, to twenty-four miles for way trains and thirty for expresses. We run four daily trains each way for through passengers and one between Cincinnati and Morrow, and three daily freights each way. These trains are all heavily loaded and yet our depots are crowded with freight awaiting its turn to be moved. We increased 9.6 per cent in passengers and 13.3 per cent in freight over 1853 and made $336,708 net, a little less than last year. "The charges which appear in our accounts, for extra advertising, solicitors and other agencies for procuring business, being wholly foreign for our usual and long-established policy, cannot but attract attention." Damn the CH&D!

1855

The Narrator. The effects of the crisis of 1854 did not last much beyond the end of that year, but the promotion of new roads does not regain its early vigor. Those which were not operating in 1854 are in for tough times. From now on the established railroads will take control of any lines that fall in trouble. The Little Miami and the C&X begin to look around among their neighbors for bargains.

The Little Miami. (To the C&X) The DX&B is a convenient link for east and west travel to Dayton and beyond to Indianapolis, and it's practically in our hands. There's no need to worry about the CC&C; we use the same complement of conductors, operatives and rolling stock, and our arrangement is permanent.

The CW&Z is still using stage coaches over a twelve-mile gap between Lancaster and Zanesville, and their three million of bonds is too much debt for that line to carry. Its engines are not in running order, it is falling in arrears on wages and its people are bordering on rebellion.

The M&C has spent six million dollars and hasn't gotten anywhere. The Pennsylvania invested $650,-000 in their stock, and may have some idea of using it for an entrance to Cincinnati.

The Zanesville and the Marietta will bear watching. What about the Ohio Central?

The C&X. That road promises to become a valuable interior channel for business out of Columbus. But the tunnel at Cambridge has fallen in and its credit is broken. The B&O has the whiphand there.

The SM&V&P. (Comes pleading to the Little Miami) If we don't get a couple hundred thousand more to build from Delaware to Crestline, we're done. Please, won't you give us a lift?

The Little Miami. (Cautiously, with a glance toward its partner, the CC&C) The existing circumstances are adverse to railroad enterprises, but the interest of our stockholders would be promoted by extending some pecuniary assistance to you. We'll lend you a locomotive, the *Power,* and we'll subscribe to another hundred thousand of your stock at sixty if the Pennsylvania will match us.

The Ohio & Mississippi. For God's sake, we need some help too. The council of Cincinnati is pretending to buy our wharf property for $500,000, because the Ohio constitution won't let the cities lend money any more. Our road is going to cost twenty millions, three times as much as Mitchell estimated, and every contractor has gone broke, one after the other.

The Little Miami. (Reflectively to the C&X) "The construction of roads, south of the Lakes, having an east and west direction, has been the means of diverting from us a portion of the business, which formerly trended to Cincinnati . . . and much of the intercourse between St. Louis and New York has taken the same course. Some of the business which has thus been diverted from our city, will be restored to its original and most direct channel, whenever the connection by railroad, between Cincinnati and St. Louis shall be established." (XIII) But the trouble is, we just can't back the O&M, because it has such a rotten reputation. It's become a jest and a byword. (Aloud to the O&M) We're sorry, but we can't do anything for you just now.

The Little Miami. (To itself, as it looks, reflectively, off toward the south) "Twenty years ago, a system of railroads was projected, to extend from . . . our northern frontier to the ocean, at Charleston, S. C. It was not difficult to foresee, even at that day, the magnitude of the interests involved in this great enterprise, embracing an avenue for the commercial interchange of the products and manufacturers of more than fifteen degrees of north and south latitude, by the shortest possible line. . . . In Ohio, the connection has been completed by several routes. . . . In the Southern States five thousand miles of railroad have been constructed. . . . South of Cincinnati, a railroad is in operation from Covington to Lexington. . . . But about one hundred and twenty miles of railway . . . remain to be made to connect . . . with some of the several railways of Tennessee which are now eagerly seeking this connection, and to unite the whole system of southern railroads through Cincinnati, with the whole web of northern, northwestern and eastern railroads." (XIII) Just as soon as the Covington & Lexington is extended to Knoxville, a man could reach, within two days, Chicago, Montreal, Boston, New York, Philadelphia, Baltimore, Washington, Charleston, Mobile, Pensacola or St. Louis. (Speaking to its stockholders)

There has been an extreme cold this year—the thermometer sinking in February to thirty degrees below zero—a drought which prevailed widely over the country and greatly diminished its resources for business, and an extensive derangement of monetary affairs. Our 41 engines ran 680,587 miles. Gross revenues of the Little Miami and the C&X were over a million dollars and we declared a ten per cent dividend, and paid it in 1853 bonds.

1856

The Little Miami. (Talking over the situation with the C&X and the CC&C) Frankly, we're worried. "Our net income has not been increased in proportion to the facilities we have afforded to the public for travel and transportation. The number of competing routes, and the eagerness of those who control them to procure business, have reduced the prices both of freight and travel below the point of just remuneration, and have obliged us to perform a large amount of service without a corresponding profit." (1st J.)

The CC&C. The representatives of the Western railroads who got together last year approved the establishment of a uniform tariff of rates. That would remove the temptation to solicit business by underbidding, and satisfy the public by making the charges on all roads equal and fair.

The Little Miami. We shall respond cordially to any such friendly demonstration. "Many of the mischiefs resulting from real or supposed rivalry between competing roads would be materially lessened, if not wholly prevented, by frank and liberal intercourse between their officers." (1st J.)

The CH&D. (Also in gloomy conference with its allies, the Mad River, the Dayton & Michigan, and the Hamilton & Eaton) We have made permanent arrangements with every road entering the Big Miami Valley to prevent strength being given to any rival project. The H&E will soon have its connection with Chicago through Logansport, and when the O&M opens up we'll take over all the traffic from St. Louis. But we've had to borrow three million dollars on our bonds, and we haven't yet been able to get a decent eastern outlet. The Junction road from Sandusky isn't at Cleveland, and the route up the Mad River to Sidney or the D&M and then over the Bellefontaine is too roundabout.

(The CH&D beckons to the Cincinnati, Wilmington & Zanesville and the Marietta & Cincinnati.)

The CH&D. The Little Miami thinks it is *the route par excellence* and acts as if it had a right to all the Cincinnati and eastern business. Do you suppose they'll ever let you have any part of it? Why, you don't even get a fair share of the track into Cincinnati; it is crowded up with the passengers and freight the Little Miami has taken away from you. Wouldn't it be better to get the disgruntled Lebanonites and all join together in building a line to Glendale, and then use our line and our station in Cincinnati?

(The Little Miami breaks into the group.)

The Little Miami. Wait just a minute before you

PASSENGER STATION OF THE LITTLE MIAMI ROAD, ON FRONT STREET NEAR THE OHIO RIVER, CINCINNATI. THE WESTERN END IS SHOWN IN THE FOREGROUND, THE TRAINS ENTERING AND DEPARTING ON THE EAST.

"I have seen many fine depots, in the east and the west—some of solid, beautiful stone—but I have seen none more spacious or convenient than this." *(Cincinnati, Columbus and Erie Railroad Guide; Anonymous; 1854.)*

decide. We have laid a double track all the way to Morrow. The M&C can have the independent use of the line from Loveland and our depot for sixty thousand a year. The CW&Z will pay $100 for each outgoing train, not less than fifty thousand yearly, and we must control the fares to Morrow. If Lebanon will raise $60,000, we'll build a branch line.

(The CH&D is instantly deserted for the Little Miami by the CW&Z and the M&C.)

The Little Miami. (Soliloquizing after they are gone) "Our income the past year has been $1,257,-735, . . . an excess of $192,455.90 over the receipts from the same sources during the previous years, being equal to about nineteen per cent. . . . The passengers have been less than the previous year. The causes of this falling off are traceable to the low stage of the Ohio River, preventing the Southern and Southwestern travel from reaching Cincinnati, during a large portion of the year, and its consequent deviation from our line of railroads terminating at Cairo and St. Louis." (1st J.) "The regularity and safety with which our trains have been run, is due chiefly to the excellent character and conduct of the persons employed in our business, and the methodical system of police established by our Superintendent. We employ none but sober, capable and respectable men and we exact from them the literal and strict observance of all our regulations." (1st J.) The total cost of the road to the end of this year is $3,286,063, and of the rolling stock, $768,035. We paid two cash dividends of $149,064, each.

1857

The Narrator. The Pennsylvania felt so confident about the future at the beginning of the year that it bought the rest of the Main Line of Works that still belonged to the State. From now on passengers can ride from Philadelphia to Pittsburgh without changing cars.

The Pennsylvania. (Waves a friendly hand to the Little Miami) You persuaded us to put that money in the SMtV&P so that they could build up to Crestline. We expected to use the line for an entrance to Cincinnati by way of your road from Springfield, but you ought to be told that our plans have changed.

The Little Miami. Our connection with Pittsburgh over the CC&C is working nicely. We've reduced passenger fares to eight dollars for first-class and to five for second; and we've pooled our rolling stock so that the CC&C furnishes sixteen cars for through freight, we furnish thirty-four, and the PFtW&C fifty, as you know.

The Pennsylvania. Good, but listen to this. We are backing the road from Pittsburgh to Steubenville, and shall subscribe half a million to put the Steubenville & Indiana through to Newark. From there the line will run in to Columbus over the Central Ohio tracks. If you come in with us you'll have a shorter haul to Pittsburgh and save the split with the CC&C.

The Little Miami. We'll have to submit that to the CC&C under our agreement. (To the CC&C) What do you say?

The CC&C. (Resignedly) What can we do, except consent? Anyway, we'll still keep your New York business. By the way, times are pretty tough. We'd feel better about it if you let us have twenty thousand to tide us over.

(The Little Miami hands over the money without a whimper.)

The Narrator. The B&O does not stand idly by while the Pennsylvania is invading Ohio. The Central Ohio feeds passengers and freight into Wheeling. The Northwestern Virginia has, after six years, just been completed to the Ohio river and the B&O is working the line with its own rolling stock. The last spike has been driven on the M&C line, and it has built a short branch down the river toward Parkersburg. The Ohio & Mississippi has won its way from Cincinnati to St. Louis. It is possible to travel, if not in the same car, at least in more or less continuous motion, from Baltimore to the Mississippi. This is something that calls for a celebration. The O&M sends invitations out broadcast over the country, while the B&O and the M&C join in with a vim.

First Eye Witness. Did you hear about the Great Railway Celebration of 1857? Our jovial company —members of the President's cabinet, senators, governors, mayors, historians, preachers and other celebrities; not to forget the ladies, whose refining influence added not a little—four hundred and fifty of us all told, left Baltimore at six in the morning of June first. "The voice of the locomotive was heard in the valleys and on the hilltops." We reached Grafton after nine that night and were hailed by a salvo of artillery and offered the hospitality of the splendid hotel there, "erected in the gothic and corinthian style of architecture." Next day, we started at early dawn and arrived in mid-morning at Parkersburg on its high bluff at the junction of the Kanawha and the Ohio. There we picked up a hundred and fifty more hungry and thirsty souls. Steam ferries lashed together puffed eight miles upstream while we discussed a sumptuous repast. At Marietta, the cannon, the martial strains of fife and drum, the flowery addresses of Governor Chase of Ohio and of Lewis Cass, Secretary of State, and of a dozen others welcomed us. The good Monongahela whiskey never once ran dry. At two in the afternoon we crossed the Muskingum in boats, boarded M&C trains, and zigzagged back and forth up the mountains on the switchbacks above the two unfinished tunnels, and so over a bumpy road to Chillicothe. That night a thousand of us were lodged in private houses—"a hearty and whole-souled specimen of hospitality." The next day we were greeted at the Little Miami depot in Cincinnati by nine hundred guests who had come over from St. Louis, and twenty thousand local citizens. The military, the Guthrie Grays and the Fulton Continentals, escorted us to Fountain Square to witness the marvels exhibited by those brand-new steam fire-engines. The town was bright with flags, banners, inscriptions and decorations. The best motto of them all, was: "A locomotive is the only good motive for riding a man on a rail." The orator most applauded was the inebriated gent, who swayed gracefully to and fro, and bellowed about the sublimity of

America, forever free from priestly and aristocratic tyranny. Fifteen hundred went along to St. Louis early next morning. Engines broke down and emergency repairs to the track held us up, but every time the trains stopped, whether at a station or in the wildwood, somebody was ready with a speech. We reached the Mississippi long after midnight, and were put to bed on four steamboats tied up to the bank. Next day we crossed the river, marched to the Fair Grounds, and heard seventeen more speakers. It was the biggest, the furtherest, and the speechinest celebration this country has ever seen.

Second Eye Witness. I went on the return party of the B&O on July 15th. *We* started from St. Louis with not more than five hundred select gentlemen—the real *bon ton*. Everything was dignity and grace and elegance. From Cincinnati we passed smoothly over the Model Road, the Little Miami, you know, to Columbus, and rode on the Central Ohio to Bellaire. Whenever the engine caused an enforced halt, a ballroom was extemporized and the band put in requisition. And then at Baltimore, what a polished reception! There was a grand procession with fireworks afterward, of course, and a banquet of a hundred dishes at the Maryland Institute. But no roaring rhodomontades, not so for us; classic discourses instead, in response to stately toasts—"The Young West—the finger of Destiny points to it"; and "The City of Cincinnati, her lap teeming with manufactures, she well adorns the coronet that graces her queenly brow." How's that for high—yes siree, high, wide and handsome?

First Eye Witness. Golly Moses! But I'll bet our crowd had more fun than you did.

The Little Miami. (To the O&M) We are going to memorialize council for a connection track on the streets in the vicinity of the river bank from your depot to ours, so that we can exchange traffic without changing cars or breaking bulk. That will help to shut off this constant diversion and direct to Cincinnati much of the business that has passed to the North.

The Narrator. The tumult and the shouting die. In August, prices on the stock exchange suddenly fell forty to fifty per cent. The country slipped faster and faster down a steep decline into an abyss of depression. The American people are again disenchanted, and in the grip of fear and despair. The great panic of 1857 is on. Why such things must be and what it means, no one can tell. The factors of the human mind which underlie economic laws are, and always will be, too infinite in number, too complex in nature and too fitful for human understanding.

One thing, however, is clear: the billion dollars or so which has been sunk in railroads in the last years can earn only forty million, and some of the investors are bound to lose. Lines like the Erie and the New York Central are locked in deadly competition with each other; others like the Mad River and the CW&Z default their bonds. The Ohio Life Insurance and Trust Company, old friend of the Little Miami, goes bankrupt, the eastern cities suspend specie payments and every private bank in Ohio closes its doors.

President Buchanan and Washington stand stupidly by, but they, at least, do not make the suffering unbearable by sanctimoniously reading moral lectures. It will take eighteen months to dispel the universal dsitrust and to get a fresh start.

The Little Miami. (Sadly, going over the books in December) For the first time our income has been less—by $46,437—than the previous year. The causes grew out of the adoption of rates of transportation considerably below the point of fair remuneration; the comparatively small amounts of shipments to the eastern markets; and the sudden and almost overwhelming commercial disasters of the country. Nevertheless, we are not down-hearted. "The prominence of our road as a part of the railway lines between Cincinnati and the East, the West and the South, is fully maintained. . . . Our valuable connections at either terminus of our respective roads, and the steadily growing business of these leading tributaries, must continually add to the value of our line and permanently secure it an eminent position in the railroad system of the country." (2nd J.)

1858

The Narrator. The railroads are learning sorrow and take stock of themselves. A committee, Helm of Pennsylvania, Powell from London, Lincoln the leader of the Cincinnati bar, and others, go over the affairs of the Marietta & Cincinnati.

The M&C. (In confidence to the committee) This road of ours has cost more than $34,000 a mile. The tunnels between Athens and Marietta and the bridge over the Muskingum have never been finished, and the ferry to Parkersburg is costly and cumbrous. We had to use the hundred thousand the Pennsylvania advanced us to stave off debts against the line west of Marietta instead of building up to Wheeling. We owe nine millions in bonds and floating debts, and we can't possibly avoid a default on our July coupons. The bondholders have a petition for foreclosure ready to file.

The Pennsylvania. (Indignantly) So you admit that you misapplied the funds earmarked to build the connection with our Hempfield road. It will cost a million or so more to put your road in any kind of shape. We're going to write off your stock and your obligations as worthless. We're done with you.

The CH&D. (Growing hungry and mean, to itself) Two hundred and twenty-five thousand in the Cincinnati, Logansport & Chicago that used to be called the Hamilton & Eaton, ten thousand in the Greenville & Miami—and nothing to show for it except a dribble of freight from Indiana. Over two hundred thousand sunk on the direct route from Hamilton to Indianapolis that looks like a dead loss. We're next door to the terminus of the O&M, but the Little Miami, a mile away, gets most of their business. We gave forty thousand to the Springfield & Columbus and the C&X stopped it at London. Those lake boats the Mad River stuck us with to the tune of a hundred thousand dollars have never earned one penny of profits. Ninety thousand more to the D&M before we get the connection this summer with the PFtW&C at Lima. We've got to apply all our undivided profits to wipe out our losses—and won't the stockholders howl?

The Little Miami. (Also to itself) Our income is derived in a great measure from through trade; the business of the country has been comparatively light, and the number of passengers is at the lowest point since 1852. Twenty-two thousand more tons of freight went east than came west—that threw things out of balance. "The gross revenues for the year were $1,200,499, being an increase over those of 1857 of $37,336, while the net income exceeds that of the previous year in the sum of $77,205, disclosing the gratifying fact of the greater experience in the management of our Roads, leading to increased economy in working them." (3rd J.) Our passenger car mileage was 1,472,346 this year, over our line, the CC&C to Cleveland, the Central Ohio to Bellaire, and the PC&C to Pittsburgh. Our cars now have spiral springs on a pad of India rubber, are beautifully varnished and upholstered and elegantly lighted by four wax candles set in carriage lamps.

1859

The C&X. (To its partner) The DX&B keeps insisting that we lease its line. It is so short and it cost so much that it will never pay. But if you say so, we'll take it for twenty years and pay the interest on its bonds.

The Little Miami. The direct earnings won't cover the outlay for rent and expenses, but the business from Dayton, Indianapolis and the West might counterbalance the deficit.

The D&W. (At the further end of the DX&B) The gauge of our road and the Indiana Central must be changed to conform to your four foot-ten before we can properly accommodate that western traffic. Will you put up the money?

The Little Miami. That means a row in the Board. Our president says contributions of that kind are bad business. The best we can do is $10,000.

(Meantime, Erasmus Gest, Receiver of the Cincinnati, Wilmington & Zanesville is whispering to a banker from the East.)

Erasmus Gest. (Showing a map) If we can get our receivership lifted and a million of stock and bonds underwritten, we'll dig a tunnel under Walnut Hills and Avondale that will place our terminus at the end of the Miami canal and next to the slaughter-houses along Deer creek. The city will contribute something and the M&C and the Lebanon people will take shares. Then we can run eastern traffic to the B&O at Wheeling, or else to Pittsburgh and interchange with the Pennsylvania, without paying charges to the Little Miami.

The Banker. You can't raise a cent in this country. But if you'll letter that map in French instead of English, we'll try it on our friends in Paris.

(The CH&D and the Mad River edge toward each other again.)

The Mad River. We have been fighting each other ever since your D&M got to Toledo. What's the use? It's not doing us a particle of good.

The CH&D. (Grudgingly.) The trouble is that we can't protect our eastern traffic so long as we have to trans-ship at Dunkirk or at Buffalo from propellers to unfriendly roads. A land and water route is bound to lose out to an all-land route.

The Mad River. We are thinking of consolidating with the Junction Road and changing our name to the Cincinnati, Sandusky & Cleveland. We are going to cancel all our arrangements with the Little Miami, arrange a division of the property jointly held, and adjust all our accounts, some of them of long standing. That connection has spelled ruin to us from the very beginning and now we're done with it forever.

The CH&D. (Struck with a sudden idea, rushes over to the SMtV&P) You have as much reason to be sore at the Little Miami as the Mad River. How would this be for a trunk line to the East? Our road to Dayton, the Mad River to Springfield, the SMtV&P to Delaware and the CC&C there into Cleveland. Our other lines and all our connections will feed traffic, and between us we'll arrange to control the fares on the lake boats. That'll stop this competition against each other and show what we can do.

(They go into a huddle and end up in complete accord.)

The Little Miami. (Feeling lonesome, doubtful about the CC&C, and consciously virtuous) The contest between the great rival lines is going to cause so great a reduction in the rates of transportation as to essentially diminish the revenue of our line. "Our

OPERATIONS AND ALLIANCES 133

rule of management has ever been to secure customers by fairness, punctuality and candor; and the result proves that such are the reliable sources of success. Other popular expedients may answer for the day, but they do not bring permanent prosperity. Allow us to say, that we are strong in the belief that the time is gradually approaching, when *our* policy will become the general railroad policy of the country—when railroads will be managed like the other great departments of business, in a spirit of candor and mutual concession—when each one will seek profit by faithful and economical management of its own legitimate business, rather than by pirating on its neighbors—when each will concede to the other its own peculiar advantages, wasting no labor or money in making war upon them—when all the popular, but discreditable devices to get business, by detraction, underbidding, etc., etc., which merely provoke retaliation, and benefit no one—will be utterly abolished—when that strict integrity, punctuality and fairness, so long the pride as well as the strength of the mercantile class, will become equally the honor of the railroad community." (4th J.)

The CH&D. (Contemptuously) We're sick and tired of your lectures.

The Little Miami. (Turns away to report to its stockholders) Our gross income this year was $1,276-754 and the net $566,934. We paid three four per cent dividends in cash. The telegraph transmitted 41,417 messages. "It enables the Superintendent to be familiar with the daily movement of trains and many of the details of business on the road, while it imparts to the officers at the heads of the several departments, an electro-telegraphic presence." An M&C locomotive ran through the back of the Cincinnati station, but missed the pier, otherwise the whole end would have fallen.

1860

The Narrator. The Little Miami finally comes to realize that, in spite of its standing and inherent worth, it must nevertheless keep the good will of its neighbors.

The Little Miami. (Holding out its hand to the CH&D) We meant all those friendly things we used to say about you. Aren't we spoiling everything with this senseless competition? Let's pool our earnings and divide them under some plan alike just and beneficial. What do you think would be fair?

The CH&D. (In the same spirit) We must each retain half of our gross earnings for expenses; then you can have sixty-nine per cent of the other half and we'll be satisfied with thirty-one.

The Little Miami. The contract shall be in force for twenty years, and as soon as the earnings increase, you shall have a larger share. If any inequalities in the division of the business should arise, or the effects are burdensome, we can restore a proper equilibrium. We'll each of us manage our own roads under our own organizations, but we'll appoint one General Ticket Agent for both lines, a joint committee will fix through rates, and we'll each charge the same fare between Cincinnati and Columbus whether by way of Dayton or Xenia.

The CH&D. That's more than fair. (With a wink) But wait just a moment before we sign up. (Calls gruffly to the SD&C and the SMtV&P) Hey you, we'll have to call off that understanding we had with you last year. Our lawyers advise us that a railroad charter gives power to make rate agreements with other roads only where they cross each other but never where they are parallel. A combination of kindred interests like this one of ours is at war with the laws of trade and against public policy.

The SD&C and The SMtV&P. (In amazement and anger) What are you talking about? The Little Miami and the C&X run parallel to you just as much as we do. You entered into a binding obligation with us, and now you are making exactly the same kind of a contract, with increased solemnity, in direct opposition to us. If one of them is illegal and at variance with the principles of the common law, why, you damn hypocrite, the other one is too.

(John W. Garrett, newly elected president of the B&O, comes on stage and looks with a masterful eye over the plains of Ohio.)

Garrett. Why Wheeling? It was a mistake, because we're shut out of Pittsburgh for good. But if we watch our chance perhaps we can grab the Central Ohio for a connection to Columbus and Chicago. The CW&Z will be up for sale in a few days. We don't want it. Our main line across Ohio will go from Parkersburg over the M&C, and after it's foreclosed and reorganized, it won't cost us much to buy control.

(The effect on the enfeebled M&C of a little encouragement from a great and powerful railroad is immediate and bad.)

The Little Miami. (Angrily to the M&C) What do you think you are trying to do? For the last six months you have been reducing rates to common points, paying drawbacks and commissions, and doing serious injury to our business. You advertise tickets to Baltimore at half the usual fare and freight on flour to Charleston at one dollar per barrel instead of one forty-five. You have set our contract at naught, and our lawyers advise us to enforce our rights by injunction, unless these just grounds for complaint are removed.

The M&C. (Contemptuously) Sue and be damned to you.

The Little Miami. That puts you off our list. (To the public in general) We solicit your patronage for our two expresses, one leaving Cincinnati at nine in the morning and the other at eleven-thirty of the afternoon. Both make connections for:

Cleveland via the CC&C, 255 miles;
Pittsburgh via the CC&C to Crestline and via the PFtW&C, 365 miles;
Pittsburgh via the S&I and the P&S, 310 miles;
Zanesville via the Central Ohio, 179 miles;
Zanesville via the CW&Z, 167 miles;
Wheeling via the Central Ohio from Columbus or the CW&Z from Marion to Zanesville and thence via the Central Ohio, 261 miles.

The Narrator. The American people have set

themselves again to exploit the resources of their great country; there is a growing prosperity that, so it seems, will never end. And yet—the South has gone along all these years serenely holding to an unshaken faith in cotton, wasting its money and exhausting its resources, so that its plantations are plastered with mortgages and its merchants loaded down with debt. A year ago, John Brown seized Harper's Ferry. This fall, Lincoln is elected President. The hatreds and stresses and ferments that have been at work for years will explode next spring in a war that will set the world new standards of waste and bloodiness.

The Little Miami. (Summing up) Last winter was very cold, and to the south of us grain crops were seriously damaged by drought, but we have had an abundant crop in the country through which the road passes. This has been our biggest year; 357,858 passengers all told, and 30,532,575 ton miles of freight, 17,385 more than last year; our earnings have been $1,289,844. Movements of freight have been very irregular this year. The increase in tonnage moved Westward was 35,944 tons and the excess 15,369. The transportation of cotton is rapidly becoming an important item. The CH&D paid us $29,157 for our share of the pooled earnings. "In the death of Capt. Strader and of the late John Kilgour, the Company has lost two of its long-tried and most valued friends." (5th J.)

THE EPILOGUE

The Narrator. In 1860 the river traffic was heavier than it had ever been. Unfortunately, the boats have been tied up every spring and summer since 1855 by low water and every winter by ice. As some fellow in Congress once said: "That Ohio creek, dried up one-half of the year and frozen the other half." At the best, travel by river is slow, circuitous and subject to interruption. Whether at normal stage or in flood, treacherous shoals, hidden snags, eddies and falling banks lie in wait for the unwary. The canal around the Falls of the Ohio at Louisville is too small and is always flooded at high water. It seems inevitable that, sooner or later, the man who backs the steamboat against the locomotive will lose.

The pattern of the eastern American railroad systems begins to show in 1860. There is a ganglion of tracks in the New England states and another between New York and Philadelphia. You have seen the railroads criss-crossing the valleys and prairies and lake terraces of Ohio during these ten years of the Fifties. The network out here, on this stage before you, is almost as closely woven as east of the Alleghanies.

Beyond to the west, Chicago, hardly worth mentioning a few years ago, has suddenly become a railroad center connected with the Mississippi at a dozen points from Prairie du Chien down to St. Louis and even Memphis. It has access to Iowa, Minnesota, the Dakotas and Nebraska. The eastern systems, the Pennsylvania, the B&O, the Erie and the New York Central that is to be, have wriggled past the mountains into Ohio, and each one is studying how to reach Chicago by backing and buying adherent roads. The streams of travel that came by river to Cincinnati are caught in midpassage, and the immense commerce of the Northwest is diverted more and more to the lines that run through northern Ohio.

Down in the South a great railroad network sprawls from the Atlantic coast into Tennessee and Alabama. There are only two roads that join the North with the South, one meandering along the seaboard and another down the Mississippi valley from Chicago. A third is building rapidly from Louisville to Nashville. But the long-delayed link between Danville and Knoxville, across a hundred and twenty miles of rough terrain, has not even been started. It seems that the immense amount of business belonging to this route must, sooner or later, attract the enterprise of capitalists.

All of this is not good for Cincinnati. The Queen City is beginning to lose her supremacy of the West and her predominance in the South.

There is also peril to the Little Miami in the machinations of a wily and determined rival close at hand. The CH&D has made up its mind to seize the traffic from the west to Cincinnati. You have witnessed its frantic efforts to secure an outlet to the east. The two roads have gone into a friendly combination, for the moment, but the end is not yet.

1861–1869

WAR, PEACE AND SURRENDER

THE usefulness and importance of the Little Miami grew greatly through most of the decade. Then suddenly, in the last days, it found itself to be just a little railroad that needed a friend.

PERSONNEL

The railroaders who had built and worked the Little Miami were almost all dead except Clement. He presented his resignation from the presidency on January 31, 1867. "After nearly thirty years' service on the railroads of Ohio," he wrote, "more than twenty-four of which have been spent upon your road in various capacities, I look back with sincere pleasure upon my personal and official intercourse with such men as Jeremiah Morrow, Jacob Strader, John Kilgour, Nathaniel Wright, John Hivling, William Lewis and early friends of the road, and I shall ever cherish a warm remembrance of the kindness, as well as a grateful and friendly recollection of the uniform regard and consideration you have manifested toward me personally and officially." He held on as a director, for nineteen years longer and faded from view, at last, in 1886.

A few of the old-timers were still left, but the last president to operate the road was an outsider and a newcomer.

HUGH JUDGE JEWETT, native of Maryland, grew to manhood and practiced law there for a year or so. At twenty-three he followed the line of the B&O out to Ohio. In 1848, thirty years old, he settled down in Zanesville, became a vice president of the State Bank in charge of the Muskingum branch, served one term on the legislature and another as U. S. District Attorney. His railroad career began as vice-president and general manager of the Central Ohio. In the bad year of 1857 he was appointed its receiver, and succeeded, by a combination of vigilance, earnest effort and judicious management, in restoring the road to popular esteem and confidence. A committee of Little Miami directors, appointed in March, 1868, to hunt a candidate for president, asked him to serve, and he was elected as soon as the Board could be called together.

Jewett had a clear, firm, even merciless mind. When the time came, after he had been barely eighteen months in office, he did not hesitate; it was he who leased the Columbus & Xenia and made the Lease of the Little Miami.

The next year he resigned, removed to Columbus, and took the presidency of the PC&StL. In July 1874, he was president of the Erie, at the highest salary ever, up to that time, paid to a railroad officer. Something of the steely nature of the man shows in his acceptance: "I have not taken charge of the road for the purpose of losing my reputation as a railroad man." He reduced the hapless six-foot gauge to standard, double-tracked the line from New York to Buffalo, enlarged the terminal at Jersey City, brought up the rolling stock, and spent fourteen millions of its earnings on improvements. In 1884 it proved too much for him; he ended up broken in health, and wrangling with his stockholders. He withdrew to rest in the Maryland countryside where he had been born, and died in 1898, a man not greatly loved, it seems, but always and everywhere respected.

JOSEPH R. SWAN, after many years as director of the C&X, was elected its president in 1861 and went on the Board of the Little Miami. He served there until 1885. His fame rests secure on his Treatise for Justices of the Peace, which has been revered, even as the ark of the covenant, by every lay jurist in Ohio, and is today in its centennial (and eighteenth) edition.

THE MANY UNKNOWN served patriotically throughout the Civil War. Some Cincinnatians felt a sympathetic feeling for the South; and, although "Uncle Tom's Cabin" had been written while Harriet Beecher Stowe was living at Lane Seminary, an anti-slavery paper had been mobbed and Wendell Phillips had been driven from stage of Pike's Opera House. The Little Miami and the C&X chose sides at once. In June, 1862, the Board required that every employee who neglected or refused to take an oath of allegiance or who by word or deed evinced disloyalty to the United States government, should be instantly dismissed.

OPERATIONS, ETC.

THE CIVIL WAR, at the outbreak, brought a sudden stagnation and temporary confusion. The river trade with the South was cut short, of course, and all the every-day currents of business were changed.

Demands for military transportation soon counterbalanced the loss of Southern business. Immediately after the outbreak, George B. McClellan, president at the time of the Ohio & Mississippi, was appointed a Major-General in command of Ohio troops, and established the headquarters of the Department of the Ohio at Cincinnati. It became a concentration point for troops, a railhead for ordnance and quartermaster's stores, the home port of a fleet of river gunboats, and the center of the U. S. Sanitary Commission for the western armies. The city was put in a state of siege to resist a threatened attack by Kirby Smith in 1862, and for several weeks the line of the Little Miami was guarded by a heavy force. Again in July of the next year Morgan raided the Ohio countryside in a semi-circle to the north and east of Cincinnati. Some of his troopers ambushed the Morrow accommodation on a curve near Miamiville, wrecked the engine with a barricade of ties, killing the fireman, and set four passenger cars afire with wheat-shocks from a nearby field.

In April, 1861, Camp Dennison on the line of the Little Miami, seventeen miles from Cincinnati, was established with General Rosecrans in command. All the infantry and most of the cavalry and artillery from the area were sent there early in the war for organization and training; later on it became a replacement camp where thousands of recruits were trained and at the last a general hospital where other thousands of sick and wounded men received treatment and care.

Regular operation of the Little Miami during the war was repeatedly made almost impossible by the insistent demands of military command. There were times when nearly the entire rolling stock was concentrated between Cincinnati and Columbus. In 1862, General Buell requisitioned an engine and all the surplus freight cars. The next year, the War Department ordered the Dayton & Union to take up fifteen miles of rails for military use elsewhere, and the Dayton & Western to grant a common use to the D&U of its Dayton bridge and part of its line. Again in 1864, ex-Governor Dennison was retained to protest at Washington against a seizure of freight and passenger cars to re-stock the Nashville & Chattanooga line. In January, 1865, for three days through a terrible cold, the Little Miami carried 17,000 soldiers of the 23rd Army Corps, enroute from the battlefield of Franklin in Tennessee, to join Grant before Richmond.

"The demands of the government for the transportation of troops and munitions of war have been promptly met," Clement said with justifiable pride in 1864, "frequently requiring the whole equipment of the roads, and interrupting our local business. It is due to the officers and employees of the companies that the Boards should state the fact that the military service has been performed with a promptness and energy which has elicited the commendation of the Chief of rail transportation of the United States." (9th J.)

The number of passengers, especially in local traffic which was for a time four times as great as through traffic, increased tremendously until at the peak in 1864 it totaled 773,024.

Equipment naturally increased in proportion to the new requirements. In 1862, 86 new freight cars were not enough. Later, the Little Miami and the C&X together owned 48 locomotives, 35 first-class passenger cars, 20 baggage, mail or express, and 714 freight cars, of which 434 were box cars. Up to the Civil War, the locomotives had all been wood-burners with huge diamond-shaped smokestacks that were supposed to arrest the sparks. The first coal-burner with a spindly stovepipe was put in use by the Little Miami in 1863.

Gross income soared to more than $2,500,000 in 1864 and was only a little less the next year; and because expenses, in spite of the enhanced cost of supplies and the occasional need of guarding the line with heavy forces, did not increase as rapidly, the net income went up by leaps and bounds for four years.

These things led to a false feeling of strength and security. "At no time," said Clement in 1862, "has the financial condition been more flourishing or rested on a better foundation."

PEACE, however, came and the evil effects of the unnatural stimulus showed up at the close of the struggle in a quick paralysis of business and a slow, painful readjustment. Passenger receipts and tonnage on the Little Miami dropped back to figures smaller even than before 1860. In 1866, earnings were cut down to one third of what they had been the year before, and the Board was forced to urge a drastic reduction in personnel.

As income drops, expenses (as we in the present day have reason to know) do not fall off in the same measure. In 1866 one dollar out of every four was still paid out for the support of the government, national, state, county, city and township, and wages were up twenty-five per cent from the 1860 level. In spite of the most rigid economy, net income was cut in half to less than $400,000 in 1866, 1867 and 1868. The costs of war must, inevitably, be paid, whether in victory or in defeat.

THE ASSETS of the Little Miami went, in nine years, from $4,852,007 up to $7,048,490.

In addition to permanent improvements, it held in 1869 securities of leased or connecting roads:

C&X stock	$519,550
C&X bonds	54,000
PC&StL bonds	200,000
Street Connection bonds	197,500
D&W bonds	22,900
Little Miami Elevator stock	20,000
Yellow Springs Hotel bonds	2,000
	$1,015,950

The C&X owned, on its own account, Central Ohio

common stock of the value of $33,314 and $20,100 of the preferred stock.

THE BONDED DEBT and CAPITAL STOCK were:

		January, 1861		December, 1869	
LM Bonds		Cincinnati Loan	$100,000	Cincinnati Loan	$100,000
		Income bonds of '51	7,000	Mortgage Bonds of '53 due 1883	1,480,000
		Mortgage bonds of 1853	1,300,000	Cincinnati Street Connection Bonds	330,000
			$1,407,000		$1,910,000
Stock		$2,981,270		$3,572,400	
C&X Bonds		Mortgage Bonds	$203,000	Mortgage Bonds due 9/1/90	$302,000
Stock		$1,490,800		$1,786,200	

Dividends were paid, in cash, twice a year throughout the period; the largest being 15 per cent in 1865, and the least, 3 per cent, in 1868. A twenty per cent stock-dividend made the shareholders whole in 1864 for the cost of double-track, locomotives, rolling stock, depot grounds and other permanent improvements which had been paid out of earnings.

THE PROPERTIES—that is, the Little Miami, 123.49 miles, and the C&X, 75.33 miles—counting in second and side tracks, together with depots, equipment and so on—were operated throughout the Sixties under the Contract of Union as if they belonged entirely to the Little Miami. The partnership was dissolved on March 18, 1869, by the perpetual lease of all the assets of the C&X, its tracks, equipment, undivided ownerships in other roads and its one-third interest, valued at $643,989, in the rolling stock, investments, cash and other assets owned jointly with the Little Miami. The rent was fixed at $125,034, sufficient to pay 7 per cent dividends on the $1,786,200 of C&X stock and interest at 7 per cent on $302,000 of its first mortgage bonds. It was also provided that, as soon the Little Miami paid more than 7 per cent in any year on its own stock, the rent should be increased until the C&X could pay 8 per cent in dividends. The separate corporate organization of the C&X was continued, of course.

The trackage of the Little Miami increased only five and three-quarter miles after 1860, and the main extension into new territory was a short branch line in Cincinnati. The raceway that carried the excess water from the terminal basin of the Miami & Erie canal down the Deer creek ravine to the Ohio river, was abandoned in 1863, and city council determined to replace it with a great sewer and a wide street. This was wholly to the liking of the Little Miami, because the main approach to its brand new depot was across Deer creek, foul with the blood and offal from the slaughter houses along its banks. Fourteen thousand dollars were spent in building a trestle and filling the gully up to street level, and the City in turn granted a right to the Little Miami to lay a track 3,095 feet up Eggleston avenue with a diverging branch 596 feet long at the farther end.

The forty-two-odd miles of the Dayton & Western and the sixteen and a half miles of the Dayton & Xenia were added during the Sixties, so that the total mileage operated in 1869 aggregated 263.13. But, if the lines were not greatly extended, much money was spent to restore the roadway worn out by wartime traffic. Over twenty-three hundred tons of new steel rail (sixty-five pounds to the yard as against the hundred and thirty in general use today) and 29,000 ties were laid down in 1864, and repairs ran up to $348,000 the next year, and to $251,000 in 1866.

BIDS FOR POWER

In 1861, the Little Miami, with its partners, was a right little, tight little railroad system in itself. It ran through a rich and diversified country between the principal city of the Middle West and towns that had come to be centers of commerce. It had the prestige of many years of outstandingly satisfactory service. The traffic up and down the line between way-stations had always been greater than any through traffic that came from other roads by interchange and favor. Morrow and especially Strader firmly believed that local business would be sufficient to sustain the Little Miami in prosperity forever and that no part of it could ever be taken away by any other line.

Change, however, was in the air, and it came fast during the Sixties. The strain of carrying on and winning the Civil War had broken down barriers and unified the northern states. Ohio was no longer a frontier; it was well-established and its farmers and manufacturers and merchants looked beyond the immediate neighborhood and afar for their markets and supplies. The steady extension of the eastern railroad systems, grown strong in money and men, west of the Appalachians, indicated the trend of the times. The future began to look bad for the little fellow that served an immediate locality.

"The lines of road in Ohio," said Clement to his stockholders in 1862, "although traversing the State in almost every direction, are most of them short ones, and form at their termini and connections petty circles of competition, thus sometimes, we fear, tempting their managers to sacrifice the interests of stockholders and the accommodation of the public. But the great evil of these petty circles of competition is, that the roads of Ohio, as against the long lines east and west of the State, have become mere detached faggots, broken, and subservient to the capricious rivalries of the lines of other States; thus occupying the unenviable position of being compelled, from their own inherent fragmentary weakness, and competitions among themselves, to actually contribute a share in the losses of foreign roads, upon traffic destined to and from other States, to the injury of the producers of Ohio, who are relatively nearer market. . . . Until a more intimate union of interests and consequent unanimity of action, can be effected among the fragmentary, through lines of Ohio, it is manifest that our roads will continue to be subservient to the shifting local changes and rivalries referred to, thus making for the Ohio roads, a capriciously high rate for transportation today, and a capriciously low rate tomorrow, to the serious injury of healthy commerce, and deterring prudent traders from risking their capital in a market that transportation rates render so uncertain. We believe the interest of the Ohio roads and the communities through which they run, would alike be benefited, in the end, by the formation of more intimate business relations between the various lines, forming portions of through routes across the State." (7th J.)

The Little Miami was faced with the problem of keeping a secure and commanding place in the railroad family. It also had a natural urge of every living organism to seize and combine and extend and dominate. With a successful business and a purse pretty well-lined with surplus funds, was it to stand waiting to be devoured or would it put up a fight?

A SOUTHERN CONNECTION was the one most needed by Cincinnati and the Little Miami, and the lack of it was, of all, the most bitterly regrettable.

Lincoln, in an early message to Congress, urged the construction of the connecting link of road with Knoxville. General Burnside, commanding the Department of the Ohio, ordered a survey made across the Cumberland plateau, but time passed and as the armies marched on to the East the enterprise lost place as a military necessity.

"The establishment of organized industry in the South," said Clement expectantly in 1865, "and the natural and regular increase of population, and products to be sent to market, will furnish our road with a healthful and reasonably profitable trade." (10th J.)

The Louisville & Nashville, completed in 1859, was

still the nearest railroad between the northern network and the great southern system. But the Louisvillians had put a million dollars into the road, and stood, wide-awake and relentless, guarding the northern gate and determined that the least possible should pass through to its rival.

In 1866, the Cincinnati Short Line, 105 miles down the south bank of the Ohio to Louisville, was finished, but it was not allowed to enter the city or even to make a belt connection. The L&N, as a matter of studied design, charged excessive rates and set up embargoes against freight from Cincinnati; its pork and its products were unloaded and piled up until they were reloaded into 5-foot gauge cars. Louisville and the L&N held all Kentucky at its mercy and waxed fat. Branch lines extended eastwardly, invaded the territory of the Kentucky Central, and in 1867 one million dollars was subscribed for a line to Knoxville, in the hope of forestalling an extension of the Kentucky Central into eastern Tennessee. In three years from 1867 to 1870, the L&N doubled the number of its freight cars and the population of Louisville ran up to over a hundred thousand.

The blue-grass country immediately south of Cincinnati fought back as best it could, and sent its fine horses and blooded stock and produce to Covington across the river. For lack of a bridge, however, all freight had to break bulk and all passengers to take fresh start at the banks of the Ohio. Roebling started one of his suspension bridges for vehicles and pedestrians in 1856, but the money gave out and the work was not resumed until 1863, nor finished until 1867.

At long last in 1868, Edward A. Ferguson, who never forgot throughout thirty-two years of active practice of law in Cincinnati the illumination of the town in 1836, formulated an opinion that, even though the Ohio constitution of 1852 forbade loans of credit, the municipality still had power to build a railroad for its own account. The legislature was induced to pass the necessary laws, and an issue of ten millions of bonds was approved ten to one. Louisville went on the warpath, of course, blocked the sale of the Central Kentucky, and held up the necessary legislation in Kentucky and Tennessee. In spite of all this, construction was started in 1873 but the Cincinnati Southern, the only municipally-owned railroad in the country was not opened to Chattanooga until March, 1880, and so too late for the Little Miami.

THE WEST was connected with the Little Miami at Cincinnati in 1860 by the Ohio & Mississippi to St. Louis, and by the Indianapolis & Cincinnati to St. Louis and Chicago over a circuitous route.

In spite of the loan of Clement and a tradition of friendship in the earlier days, the Little Miami could not retain a fair share of the business of the O&M. The difference in gauge of the two lines had something to do with this, but the main reason was that the CH&D station was almost next door to the O&M terminus. In any case, within the next six years, the O&M, like the Marietta & Cincinnati, was captured by the Baltimore & Ohio, to become the B&O Southwestern of today, extending the system into the Mississippi Valley.

The I&C ran into the Cincinnati at first over the O&M tracks with a reducing third rail and into its depot, but, finding joint use with a competitor distasteful, broke away and organized the Cincinnati & Indiana in 1861 to build a separate entrance. The Little Miami jumped at the chance to make a fresh alliance, loaned $25,000 and subscribed for $100,000 out of $400,000 of the bonds of the new company, on condition that its station should be located east of the O&M. The O&M protested, of course, but the Little Miami went ahead regardless, and bid 75 for a majority of the stock. The I&C bought the Cincinnati end of the Whitewater canal, let the water out, laid its tracks in the bed, and built a station in the terminal basin just beyond Western Row. This made trouble in two ways: the disgruntled stockholders of the canal brought suit and held things up for a while and the depot was always flooded every time the river reached a fifty-five foot stage.

Within a year or so afterward, the Little Miami and the C&I secured permission from Council to lay a single track, 2.49 miles long, starting at the I&C tracks and running along Water Street, across the public river landing and down Front Street to the Little Miami depot. It was agreed that the roads should share equally in the cost of construction, and pay expenses of operation in proportion to use. The Little Miami undertook to lay the track, and financed the work with $250,000 of six per cent bonds jointly guaranteed by both roads, and $218,037 in cash out of its own pocket.

"The facilities," said Clement in explaining the

spending of the money in 1864, "for the receipt and delivery of warehoused freights along the line of the connection will add greatly to the accommodation of shippers and consignees, materially diminish the expense of handling, and naturally invite the establishment of warehouses, and transportation therefrom upon the lines of the companies. Practically it will be an extension of freight depot facilities penetrating into the city, inducting private enterprise to foster and accommodate the business of the roads." (9th J.)

The right of way was made perpetual in 1867, and Council gave all other roads entering the city from the west the privilege of using the line upon payment of tolls. The cars had to be hauled by mules in daytime but steam power was tolerated after dark. The Connection track is still in constant service and has carried an immense volume of traffic across the city.

INDIANA TRAFFIC fed into the Little Miami at Xenia over the Dayton & Western.

The D&W ran into difficulties in 1861; for bond issues, like other curses, come home to roost. Three hundred thousand dollars of seven per cent first mortgage bonds went to default and the holders refused to wait any longer. Two hundred and fifty thousand dollars of a second issue fell due in 1864 and $150,000 more of a third in 1864, but there was no money in sight to pay any of them.

Meantime, the Columbus & Indiana westwardly through Urbana and Piqua was almost completed. In July, 1862, Clement warned the Little Miami directors that it was proposed to connect this road with Richmond, and that the D&W would lose the business of the Indiana Central. The word came too late for the Little Miami to prevent construction. The Board immediately appointed a committee to buy $100,000 of Indiana Central stock, but before this could be done, the Indiana Central had, on March 9, 1863, dissolved its partnership with the D&W.

Quick action was imperative. The D&W rushed into a contract for the use of the Richmond & Miami tracks into Richmond. Three days later, on March 12, 1863, the D&W leased its properties to the C&X for five years. The next spring the Little Miami (with the C&X, DX&B and D&X), the Columbus & Indiana, the Richmond & Covington and the Indiana Central made an agreement to charge uniform rates between Columbus and Indianapolis, whether the traveller desired to go via Piqua or via Dayton, to "treat the business and traffic of both with equal fairness and equality," not to employ solicitors, runners, or other agents, and to distribute the net earnings fifty-two and one half per cent to the Little Miami and forty-seven and one half to the Columbus & Indiana. This done, the Little Miami sold out the Indiana Central shares and it was allowed to merge with the Columbus & Indiana.

The Little Miami soon found that it must carry, as dead weight, all the obligations of the D&W. Accordingly, the delinquent bonds were combined in 1864 in a new issue of $738,000—$275,000 at seven per cent and $463,000 at six per cent—and the entire use and control of the properties were perpetually leased to the Little Miami for enough to pay the interest. It was provided that, as soon as the Little Miami had redeemed the bonds, the rent should be reduced to five cents a year, and the title to the properties conveyed on demand.

Meanwhile, during 1863 and 1894, the Little Miami and the C&X together bought all but $2,000 of the Dayton, Xenia & Belpre bonds for $397,500, and 3,664 of its shares at two dollars per share. The line was sold in foreclosure in January, 1865, two-thirds to the Little Miami and one-third to the C&X.

After 1866, things took a turn for the worse. The CH&D bought an interest in the Eaton & Hamilton which ran into Richmond with the D&W over the tracks of the Richmond & Miami, and in 1869 the E&H was extended to Chicago and leased to the CH&D. In addition to this, the Cincinnati & Indianapolis Short Line starting at Hamilton began construction.

At the first the management of the Little Miami expected that the business of the D&W would counterbalance the deficits. In all, more than half a million of capital was spent in trying to hold a part of the Indiana traffic, and the loss in operations over a period of five years totalled $137,000.

LEBANON, in despair of a railroad connection over the Little Miami, organized the Cincinnati, Lebanon & Xenia, and began grading a right-of-way. The venture fell into receivership, and in March, 1864, the roadbed was sold to the Little Miami for $3,000, on the understanding that, if the people of Lebanon would subscribe $35,000, it would be completed and joined to the main line. The subscriptions were later raised to $60,000, but the old difficulties broke out again, and in December, 1866, the Little Miami reconveyed to the CL&X. In later years the Lebanonites went ahead on their own resources, to enter Cincinnati by a short tunnel under Walnut Hills and down the ravine of Deer creek to the end of the Miami & Erie canal.

THE NORTHEASTERN OUTLET of the Little Miami through Columbus and over the CC&C to the Lake Shore was so satisfactory and valuable all around, that in the early Sixties it seemed likely to last forever. The CH&D also was cooperating peacefully for the moment. "Nothing has occurred," said Clement at the end of the year, "to disturb the friendly and intimate relations of the companies. There is no reason to doubt that all the beneficial results anticipated by the friends of the arrangement will be attained." (6th J.)

But disturbance came quickly. The Springfield, Mt. Vernon and Pittsburgh went into a quick decline after it had been jilted by the CH&D in 1860. The property was sold at foreclosure in January, 1861, and the purchaser offered it to the Little Miami for $150,000. The road had value as a short cut through Springfield to the CC&C, and might at any time again succumb to the wiles of a rival. Just as the directors decided somewhat tardily to negotiate further, word came that the CC&C had bought the fifty miles between Springfield and Delaware right from under the nose of the Little Miami. A committee was instantly instructed to find out what the CC&C wanted for a half-interest. It was too late; the CC&C refused, point-blank, to sell.

The Mad River, now known as the Sandusky, Dayton and Cincinnati, had been jilted at the same time and was in no better state. The Little Miami, smarting under its loss of the SMtV&P, opened dealings with the bondholders of the SD&C to lease the road at a hundred thousand a year, so as to have a compensating outlet of its own from Springfield. The CH&D woke up at once and demanded an amendment to the contract of 1860 providing that if either party leased a connecting road the other might choose whether or not to participate in the lease.

The Little Miami then asked the CC&C for a conference on a plan to consolidate by a contract of permanent union. In October, 1862, a joint draft of an agreement was submitted and approved by the directors. A few months later, however, in April of the next year, the contract was rescinded by mutual agreement, apparently because each one feared that it might eventually be mastered by the other. Instead, the existing arrangment of a partnership with equal control was continued for five years longer. The joint earnings of both roads from passengers and freight, rent of tracks and use of depots were aggregated, fifty per cent retained for expenses and the balance divided on the basis of mileage, forty-seven per cent to the Little Miami and fifty-three to the CC&C. Agreements between the CC&C, the Lake Shore and the Bellefontaine and between the Little Miami, the

Central Ohio and the Steubenville & Indiana were authorized, and equalization of fares provided.

The CH&D might be imagined as standing by, meantime, biting its nails in fear and suspense. Relief, however, was at hand; the Erie, "that Lion of Railroads" as one of its admirers once called it, having just escaped with considerable loss of kudos from its most recent receivership, took over the Atlantic & Great Western. This other feeble monarch after dawdling about for ten years had at last crawled from Salamanca through Jamestown, Meadville, and into Ohio as far as Galion. There it was halted, unable to raise the money to build the rest of the four hundred miles to Dayton. The CH&D, bursting with the hope of gaining, finally and in what seemed to be good company, an outlet to the East, was inspired to present a set of "Confidential Proposals" to the Little Miami, the C&X and the CC&C, suggesting that they all merge under the name of "The Atlantic & Great Western, Western Division," and, joining up existing lengths of track, operate a six-foot route from Galion through Delaware, Springfield and Dayton to Cincinnati, where the CH&D would hook in with its nearby neighbor, the O&M. This was, in part at least, a revival of the same plan that the CH&D had concocted in 1859 and immediately ditched in 1860. The idea was now to run wide gauge rolling stock from the Atlantic ocean at New York, without transshipment, to the Father of Waters at St. Louis.

Two directors of the Little Miami voted no, but six were for acceptance. People were still of two minds as to whether combinations between parallel roads violated the principles of the common law. Railroad men knew that cutthroat competition leads to starvation and ends in bankruptcy, and had found agreements to pool earnings and divide profits an effective form of self-discipline that kept rates at a decent level. Others, usually outsiders and self-seekers, argued that no man could be trusted not to overcharge and to cheat, and demanded government control. Unhappily they were vindicated by the chicanery and dishonesty of those unscrupulous railway executives who, during the Seventies and the Eighties, manipulated securities, watered stock, corrupted public officials, discriminated and gave secret rebates, underpaid labor, and charged every penny the traffic could possibly bear. In the effort to cure such abuses, federal supervision and regulation by political careerists has now progressed to the point of putting every American railroad in a straightjacket.

However that may be, the scheme of the CH&D turned out to be impossible. One requirement was control of the SD&C from Springfield to Dayton, and when the Little Miami made the first move to carry out the pending deal, the Boston bond-holders not only withdrew their offers, but insisted on a complete divorce of all interests that had been held in common. Another was that the tracks of the SMtV&P into Springfield should be used by the combination, and the CC&C refused to join in or to allow any one a share in its Delaware branch. The CH&D perforce, gave it all up and started negotiations anew with the A&GW.

"The Cincinnati, Hamilton & Dayton Railroad

Company have, in accordance with its interest," Clement announced at the end of 1863, "agreed to place upon its track a third rail . . . thus giving at Dayton to the Atlantic & Great Western Company Eastward bound business, which has gone from Dayton, via Xenia, to Columbus. This will of course divert from the LM & C&X a considerable business, but must be acquiesced in as, on the whole, proper. The A&GW Co. will of course place upon its line a Cincinnati day express and a Cincinnati night express train. It is believed that this can be done without any unprofitable or unfair rvalry between the CH&D or the A&GW and our line; without materially impairing our earnings, and without disturbing our existing relations." (8th J.)

The two went along together cordially enough for a couple of years longer. The Little Miami exercised its choice not to participate in the Dayton & Michigan lease without ruffling the CH&D, and directed the D&W to grant a joint use of the bridge over the Big Miami and of the Richmond & Miami tracks to the CH&D, so that its connection to Chicago might be completed.

The third rail was laid and ready for the trains in March, 1865. That year the Erie in a moment of mushroom prosperity earned over fifteen millions of dollars. "This great traffic" said the officers of the A&GW to the CH&D, "passes through your gates and you have widened them to receive it and the proper tribute it brings with it." Such a sudden flood of money poured into its treasury that, whereas the Little Miami had paid over more than a hundred thousand dollars in the accounting of 1864, the CH&D, instead, made the payment in 1866.

In the same period, the net income of the Little Miami fell off sharply, mostly, of course, because the end of the war and the change in the times, but also because it had lost some part, at least, of its eastern traffic to the CH&D. To make matters worse, the Little Miami was required to pay and in the future would be charged under the contract of 1860 with the greater part of the current interest on the cost to the CH&D of the third rail, which had mounted from an estimate of nine hundred thousand dollars to a million and a half. It was too much; the tie between the two broke under the strain in March, 1866.

"The contract between the companies and the Cincinnati, Hamilton & Dayton Railroad Company," said Clement, "has been terminated by mutual consent, the same having practically ceased by the intervention of the Atlantic & Great Western Co." (11th J.)

To finish the tale: The A&GW badly financed and miserably run from London by its promoter and virtual owner, James McHenry, was in receivership again in 1867, and the next year it was leased, body, soul and breeches, to the Erie. The dog-fight for the Erie, between Vanderbilt, Drew, Gould and Fisk, which to this day stands a crying shame to any right-minded American, ended, as such things go, in insolvency and the repudiation of every obligation. The CH&D, a mere pawn out in the west, was thrown aside. The management of the Little Miami could thank its stars that circumstances, although certainly not foresight, had saved it from the same disaster.

A last staggering blow came in May, 1868. A month before the expiration of the contract for joint operation the CC&C, without the consent or even the knowledge of the Little Miami, suddenly merged with the Bellefontaine line, as the Cleveland, Columbus, Cincinnati & St. Louis. The old alliance was thereby abrogated, although, for some years to come, through freight and passengers were still exchanged on a fifty-fifty basis and fares divided according to mileage traveled. Even this ceased when the Cincinnati & Cleveland, incorporated in 1870, was built by the Little Miami's old engineer, Shoemaker, at the instance of Cornelius Vanderbilt, and became a link in the New York Central-Big Four system.

The interpayments during the Sixties, between the Little Miami and the CH&D and the CC&C were:

	LM to CH&D	CH&D to LM	LM to CC&C	CC&C to LM
1861	$ 25,673		No contract	
1862	49,538			
1863	49,809			$12,123
1864	107,695		$ 6,596	
1865	18,987		44,997	
1866		$18,078	10,687	
	Contract Terminated			
1867				7,407
			Contract Expired	
Totals	$271,702	$18,078	$62,280	$19,530

It thus appears that the Little Miami had paid out of its current earnings almost three hundred thousand dollars in a few years on its northeastern outlet—without either protecting it or keeping it.

WAR, PEACE AND SURRENDER 165

THE PITTSBURGH CONNECTION from Columbus was in 1860 a hookup of four weak links that threatened to break every so often. The Pennsylvania undertook the main responsibility, but the Little Miami shared, in measure, in keeping the twenty miles of the Central Ohio to Newark and the Steubenville & Indiana running.

It began in 1861 with a temporary loan of $15,000 to the S&I for the bridge over the Ohio. The next year, the road went into receivership and the Pennsylvania suggested to the Little Miami to buy $200,000 of first mortgage bonds held by a subsidiary of the Pennsylvania, and thereby control the reorganization. The bonds were taken up in lots of $25,000 at something below par.

The Central Ohio, anticipating a breakdown, came secretly to the Little Miami in 1863 and asked it to redeem $400,000 of third mortgage bonds from the clutches of the B&O, offering in return a half interest in the line between Columbus and Newark. The price was too big for the Little Miami, but the Pennsylvania put up the money and the purchase was made. Shortly after, the rest of the Central Ohio was sold in foreclosure to the B&O, but the stretch between Newark and Columbus is still jointly used by the two roads.

The S&I was in hot water again in 1865, and the Little Miami at the request of the Pennsylvania made another temporary loan of $50,000.

These investments were beyond question worth the money. The two roads together with the Pennsylvania afforded an outlet to the eastern sea-board that could not be blocked by any other rival. The business thus assured promised to offset the diversion to the CH&D and the Bellofontaine that began in 1867.

Meanwhile, the traffic from the west that was passing north of Cincinnati, grew year by year. It was too tempting for a pirate like Jim Gould, and when he came to the presidency of the Erie in 1868, he tried, regardless of its bargain with the CH&D, to steal the St. Louis connection of the Pennsylvania by putting down a third rail on the Columbus, Chicago & St. Louis westwardly from its junction with the A&GW at Urbana. The Pennsylvania was able to rescue its partner by taking a perpetual lease. Without an instant's delay, Gould pounced on the Pittsburgh, Ft. Wayne & Chicago, and bought a majority of its stock. The Pennsylvania suceeded in beating him off again by getting the legislature to pass and the governor to sign, all within thirty-five minutes, a bill classifying the directors of the PFtW&C, so that Gould could elect only one-fifth of the Board and must wait three years to get control of the management.

The Pennsylvania thereafter took steps to protect its line between Columbus and Pittsburgh from other raids by merging the several companies. The Pittsburgh, Cincinnati & St. Louis, sometimes called the "Panhandle," because it crosses the northward-reaching strip of West Virginia, and later the Lessee of the Little Miami, came into being. The Pennsylvania held $5,633,450 of the securities of the new company, while the Little Miami kept only a paltry minority interest of $200,000 in its bonds.

WAR, PEACE AND SURRENDER 167

OTHER POSSIBLE OUTLETS passed forever beyond the control and influence of the Little Miami toward the end of the Sixties.

The Cincinnati & Zanesville was an early casualty. In the words of its president, Erasmus Gest: "It had not sufficient pecuniary success for payment of maintenance and interest."

After a sell-out and reorganization in 1863, Gest had the nerve to ask the Little Miami for the price on a half interest in the line from Morrow to Cincinnati. Being put firmly back in place, he renewed the old bluff of building an independent entrance, double-track this time. The Zanesville thereupon folded up again, and was sold to the Pennsylvania for $807,000 of its delinquent bonds.

The Marietta road did not linger on to share, as a paying guest, the line from Loveland to the Cincinnati depot. Garrett of the B&O was busy picking up its shares at a discount. Early in 1866, just as soon as he got a majority, notice was given to the Little Miami that the contract, which brought in $5,000 each month, would be terminated within two years. The C&M began to pick up rights of way for an independent entrance through the northern and western outskirts of Cincinnati. Tracks from Loveland to Winton Place were laid in 1867, and from that point the B&O trains passed over the CH&D to a junction with the Ohio & Mississippi. Thus all the hope of the Little Miami of sharing in any part of the traffic from St. Louis via Cincinnati to points in northern Ohio was ended; it continued, as a matter of course, up the line of the CH&D.

168   THE LITTLE MIAMI RAILROAD

SURRENDER

The end came in 1869. Jewett saw and understood and faced the facts with cold courage.

"Since your last annual meeting," he reported to the stockholders in December, "many important changes have taken place in the railroad system of the country, changes involving in many particulars, the immediate interests of this Company."

"The consolidation of the lines of road between Buffalo and Chicago became the subject-matter of serious consideration. So long as the companies owning the roads between Cleveland and Buffalo had no interests west of Cleveland, this Company had no reason to doubt that by continuing the policy which it had always pursued toward those companies in connection with the Cleveland and Columbus Company, the relations heretofore existing would continue, and our road would continue to be used by them as their line to Cincinnati, the South and the Southwest, but when their interests became identified with the roads west of Cleveland, it was not difficult to foresee that a state of things might arise in which their interests might be adverse to those of this Company, and in which this Company, without a large expenditure of money, would be powerless for its own protection. Shortly after this consolidation, and before the combined companies had given any evidence of what might be expected in the future, the Pittsburgh, Cincinnati and St. Louis Company, the immediate ally and representative of the Pennsylvania Company, became the owner by purchase of the Cincinnati &

WAR, PEACE AND SURRENDER 169

Zanesville road, with arrangements already made for the extension of the road from Zanesville to Dresden, there connecting with its own line of road, thus bringing the road of that Company within thirty-six miles of the City of Cincinnati. To wait for the completion of the road between Zanesville and Dresden, was in the opinion of your Board of Directors, but to wait until the alternative was presented of giving to the Pittsburgh, Cincinnati and St. Louis Company an unrestricted right to use your road between Morrow and Cincinnati or the building of an independent road between Morrow and Cincinnati.

"The Baltimore and Ohio Company had already obtained the control of the Cincinnati & Marietta road and adopted that as their Cincinnati connection. The Erie Company had, in like manner, such control as it desired over the Hamilton & Dayton road, and had its independent Cincinnati connection.

"Under these circumstances it became a serious question for those in charge of our property and interests to determine what was proper, best and wise for them to do, and giving to the subject that consideration its importance demanded, they could not doubt that their true line of duty led to an alliance of some kind with the Pennsylvania interests, and thus impressed, interviews and negotiations followed, which have resulted in a lease of your road to the Pittsburgh, Cincinnati and St. Louis Company. . . ."

To sum up:

The great flow of trade that once passed up and down the Ohio had dwindled down to a mere thread after the Civil War. The economy of the Southland, ravaged and despoiled by war, lay in hopeless ruin. When, if ever, it was restored the steam boat would no longer prevail against the railroad. The Knoxville connection had never been built; the Cincinnati Southern existed only in the opinion of a lawyer; and the nearest railroad ran through the hateful city of Louisville.

The western traffic was, in large part, lost. The I&C was connected with the Little Miami and friendly, but the direct route to St. Louis had gone over to a hostile camp. The commerce of central Indiana might keep the D&W and possibly one other road fairly busy but it was not sufficient for three or four of them. Worst of all, the vast Northwest now belonged to Chicago, and all the trunk lines from the West to the East passed to the north of Cincinnati.

The CC&C, the old-time outlet to the northeast, had been captured by the New York Central, and would never again be helpful as it had been for so many years. The Erie now controlled a line that thrust into the southwestern corner of Ohio. The CH&D, whether it kept on with the A&GW or not, would always be a bitter, if not a sinister, competitor for eastern business.

The alliance with the Pennsylvania still remained firm, but the Little Miami had no real control over the lines beyond Columbus, and no recourse whatsoever, if, in the fast-changing order, the roundabout route to the east should be abandoned by the Pennsylvania for a short-cut through Zanesville.

The territory between Cincinnati, Dayton, Springfield and Columbus yielded a goodly amount of passengers and freight, of course. Still the monopoly did not seem so unassailable as it was thought to be, since the M&C had started to build its own entrance into Cincinnati; and another road might sometime tap the very heart of the demesne with a feeder. Then, as the lines running north and east from Cincinnati, more or less parallel, were gathered one by one into the great Eastern systems, it became painfully clear that the Little Miami could no longer stand alone, could not forego all through traffic and live on its local traffic alone. And, by way of a warning example, the eighteen miles of original track between Xenia and Springfield which was not used as a through line had come to be almost as useless as a vermiform appendix.

* * * * *

Here ended, then,
Progress this way. When, in the very nick
Of giving up, one time more, came a click
As when a trap shuts—you're inside the den!

CHILDE ROLAND TO THE DARK TOWER CAME.

AND WHY? The answer is clear. A railroad, like every other organization of human beings from football teams to totalitarian governments, is no abler or stronger or greater than its leaders—and mostly one single master. The Little Miami built itself and did its work as a common carrier under as proficient and honest a set of men as ever ran a railroad. What it lacked was a big boss like John Edgar Thomson of the Pennsylvania or John W. Garrett of the B&O, a raider like Jim Gould, an unscrupulous financier like Daniel Drew, or a merciless dictator like Cornelius Vanderbilt. With any one of these in charge, any one of the bids for power that the Little Miami made throughout the Sixties might well have resulted in complete dominion throughout Ohio and even beyond; with nothing but a railroad operator, however able, at its head, it was doomed.

THE SURRENDER was to the inevitable. If it be tragedy that all things human must have an end, that

> *The sceptre, learning, physic must*
> *All follow this and come to dust—*

then the story of the Little Miami is tragic. I, for one, believe not. It had fulfilled a purpose and it had served a human need. Surrender, when hope is gone, is not shameful; nor is there any sadness in death at the end of the day.

1870-1936

THE LEASE—EASE WITH DIGNITY

THE Lease, dated February 23, 1870, demised to the Pittsburgh, Cincinnati & St. Louis Railway Company, for a term of 99 years from December 1, 1869, renewable forever, all right, title and estate in the Little Miami railroad from Cincinnati to Springfield, in the Cincinnati connection track, in all rights of way and real estate along in the line, in the Dayton, Xenia & Belpre, in the Dayton & Western and Richmond & Miami, and in the Columbus & Xenia, in all locomotives, freight, passenger, baggage and hand cars, and other rolling stock, in all shop machinery, tools, furniture, supplies and other chattels, and in all stocks, bonds, credits and money, owned by the Little Miami. (Sec. 1.)

The Lessee also received 47 locomotives, 35 passenger, 20 baggage and 714 freight cars of various kinds, and securities of the par value of $1,154,550, including:

The Lessee's own bonds	$200,000
C&X stock	519,550
C&X bonds	54,000
Street Connection bonds	197,500
D&W bonds	24,000
LM 1853 bonds	33,000

The Lessee agreed to pay all current debts of the

Little Miami, the interest on its bonds and all taxes and assessments as well, and to maintain the lines, the rolling stock, etc., as if it owned them. (Sec. 5.) The rent was $480,000 per year, in quarterly installments of $120,000, enough for eight per cent dividends on a total of $6,000,000 of Little Miami and C&X stock. (Sec. 6.)

The Little Miami agreed either to pay the outstanding principal of its 1853 first mortgage bonds amounting to $1,480,000 and its $100,000 Cincinnati loan, or to renew them with 90-year six per cent bonds. The Lessee agreed to pay interest charges to the holders of the bonds and any renewal bonds, or an equal amount to the Little Miami if it should redeem. (Sec. 9.)

Section 10 is important; it provides that "all additions of locomotives, real estate, second track, sidetracks, depots, shops and other permanent improvements necessary for the present or future increase of traffic," shall be authorized by concurrent resolution and purchased by the Lessee. In repayment therefore, the Little Miami must issue seven per cent bonds, secured by second mortgage and exchangeable for capital stock, on which the Lessee must pay the interest or the dividends if converted.

The Little Miami is required to keep up a corporate organization, and the Lessee to pay $5,000 yearly for current expenses. (Sec. 12.)

The Pennsylvania Railroad Company guaranteed payment of the rent and performance of all covenants by the Lessee. (Sec. 16.)

The Lease was signed by Hugh J. Jewett, President,

attested by Charles P. Cassilly, Secretary, for the Little Miami Railroad Company, and signed by Thomas L. Jewett, President, for the Lessee, and by J. Edgar Thomson, President, for the Pennsylvania.

On August 28, 1890, the Pennsylvania, Cincinnati & St. Louis Railroad Company, the original Lessee, was merged with the Chicago, St. Louis and Pittsburgh Railroad Company, the Cincinnati and Richmond Railroad Company, and the Jeffersonville, Madison and Indianapolis Railroad Company under the name of The Pittsburgh, Cincinnati, Chicago and St. Louis Railway Company.

Shareholders of the Little Miami owning 33,896 shares voted unanimously in favor of the Lease. The Pennsylvania stockholders were not so well pleased. An investigating committee, appointed at the annual meeting in 1874 after the death of J. Edgar Thomson, which opened a career to critics, condemned the management generally for a wasteful outlay of money, and estimated a loss of $500,000 a year from the operation of the PC&StL.

PROPERTIES AND BETTERMENTS

At the end of 1869, the total investment of the Little Miami in its road, 196.65 miles in length, including leased trackage, real estate, depots, etc., was $3,995,165, and in rolling stock and machinery, including a wharfboat on the river, $1,065,968. As the traffic increased and the art of railroading improved great sums were spent by the Lessee in betterments and added to capital account. In December, 1936, after sixty-six years, the total investment had

176 THE LITTLE MIAMI RAILROAD

A BETTERMENT OF 1907 UNDER SECTION 10 OF THE LEASE. ENGRAVED VIGNETTE ON THE SPECIAL GUARANTEED BETTERMENT STOCK CERTIFICATE.

increased about twelve millions up to $16,909,843. Equipment, meantime, fell off a hundred thousand or so because of outdated machinery, not modernized or replaced.

There were squabbles, of course, as to the character and cost of some of the betterments. The Little Miami directors exercised a constant vigilance in safeguarding the interests of the stockholders, often suspended approval of purchases or payment for lack of proof, and on occasion refused point-blank to concur in resolutions for a proposed betterment. In 1889, for instance, they balked at the price of the Cincinnati depot, and in retaliation the Lessee withheld payment of the rent until the Little Miami had to borrow money to pay dividends and interest. Again, in 1892, the Little Miami insisted it would not pay betterments on the C&X which had been piling up since 1890, and the PCC&StL brought suit in the Superior Court of Cincinnati for $65,426.60. The case was fought through the Superior Court of Cincinnati by Judson Harmon, but the Little Miami was held liable in General Term.

In 1923, the Lessee presented claims of $864,592 accumulated from 1918 to 1921. Many of the items had never before been recognized as betterments under Section 10 of the Lease, but were arbitrarily held to be permanent improvements by the Interstate Commerce Commission, so that their cost was not chargeable to current expense but must be placed in capital account. The dispute between the Lessee and the Little Miami was, this time, settled in conference, without litigation. The practical interpretation of

Section 10, established by a course of conduct over many years, was revoked, and the Little Miami, yielding to paramount authority of the Commission, was forced to issue irredeemable securities for improvements which could not in reason be said to be permanent.

B ETTERMENTS TO THE LITTLE MIAMI were more extensive and more costly than those on all the leased roads put together.

The first railroad bridge to cross the Ohio river started in 1870 from the Kentucky shore to land at a point just west of the Little Miami depot. The approaches were to extend up Eggleston avenue in expectation that railroads entering the city from the west might use the bridge from tracks laid along the canal bank. This plan was not to the liking of the Pennsylvania, and a loan of a million, four hundred thousand dollars resulted in a complete change. The Little Miami persuaded City Council to vacate Kilgour street and Eggleston avenue, between Pearl and the river, and the Lessee, with the Bridge Company, bought all privately-owned land in the intervening blocks. The Bridge Company conveyed its titles to the Little Miami for $348,517 and the Lessee for $204,483, all paid in stock under the betterment clause. The Little Miami leased back a strip near Butler street for piers and ramps, and was granted a perpetual right to cross the bridge.

On that part nearest the bridge, the new passenger station, depot shed, baggage building and freight depot of the Little Miami were located in 1880. The

Pearl street depot was pointed out for years as a grand and opulent structure. The total cost of the terminal was first estimated at less than $150,000, but what with the rearrangement of tracks and one thing or another, the Lessee spent over $238,000. There was a row, of course, but the Little Miami was forced to compromise for $200,000.

In 1884, the city turned Indian-giver and ordered the tracks removed from Eggleston avenue. The Lessee resisted and eventually the Supreme Court decided that the grant, whether valid or not, could not be revoked by the city.

The Attorney General of Ohio, however, brought suit in the Supreme Court to oust the track, and the grant was held void because it had not been approved by the state. The Lessee thereupon leased from the Canal Commissioners the right of way up Eggleston avenue and the strip between Pearl street and the river on which the new station was located at a yearly rent calculated at six per cent on $157,000. The Legislature later sold the strip outright in 1896 for $57,000, but the lease of the Eggleston avenue trackage is still in force.

In 1905, $600,000 was spent in elevating the Cincinnati tracks, and in 1916, $289,500 more. In 1907, the car-yard at Undercliff nearby was bought and improved for $276,000. The Pearl street station became, every year, more out of date and shabby. It was kept because there southern traffic was interchanged by the Pennsylvania and the Louisville & Nashville which now owned the Newport bridge. In 1916, the passenger platforms had to be extended at a cost of $206,000 to take care of much longer modern trains. Finally, in 1929, the Lessee joined with all the other railroads in the present Union Terminal on the western side of the city, and the old depot, as well as the Torrence road station at the foot of East Walnut Hills, were abandoned.

THE CINCINNATI STREET CONNECTION is wholly owned by the Little Miami. At the date of the Lease, $190,000 of first mortgage bonds were outstanding, but the Little Miami held $60,000 of them and all of the $275,000 second mortgage bonds. In 1871, the agreement with Cincinnati & Indiana was changed so that thenceforth the Little Miami paid sixty per cent of the operating deficit, but in 1877, the Indianapolis, Cincinnati & Lafayette, which had become the virtual owner of the C&I, refused to meet its share of the losses and the bond interest, and upon reorganization in 1880 by its president, M. E. Ingalls, it repudiated all liability. The Lessee, in due course, redeemed $190,000 of outstanding bonds at maturity.

Betterments chargeable to the Cincinnati Connection track have been: in 1889, purchase of property on Smith Street for $171,750; in 1893, lots at the Northeast corner of Broadway and Front street, for $132,467; in 1903, purchase of property near Broadway and Second and Broadway and East Front street for $300,000; and in 1916, purchase of additional land at Augusta, Smith and Front streets for $105,000.

The DX&B is owned outright by the Little Miami

and the C&X jointly, and the corporation has long since gone out of existence. The betterments, carried in the 1936 statement for some obscure reason in two separate accounts, were $412,285 and $1,170,508, or a total of $1,582,793. This covered the cost of relaying a miserably constructed road from end to end, and the elevation of the Dayton tracks.

The C&X is still, of course, under lease to the Little Miami, and its 8 per cent dividends are paid out of the rent received by the Little Miami. $248,000 of its outstanding bonds were redeemed by the Pennsylvania before maturity on September 1, 1890, and together with $54,000 worth, were turned over by the Lessee to the Little Miami. The C&X, however, in spite of the stipulation in the lease, refused in 1900 to issue renewal bonds. The old bonds are still held, in expectation that some day they will be exchanged for the interest of the C&X in the DX&B and the D&W.

The C&X has kept up its corporate organization in much the same way as the Little Miami, and its directors have been just as meticulous in protecting its interests. The Pennsylvania Railroad, however, has been buying the shares,—it paid the Little Miami $115 per share for 110 shares—until now less than eight per cent remains in the hands of the public.

The Little Miami paid up to 1937, a total of $2,705,371 for betterments to the C&X. Double tracking in 1904 and 1905 from Wilberforce, the seat of the negro university near Xenia, to Florence cost $298,203; and in 1912, from Alton to Glade Run, $279,100. In 1908, $259,951 was spent on elevation of tracks at Columbus.

Upon the erection of the Columbus Union depot, a block of stock in the depot company was issued to the Lessee, subject to such uses and trusts as the C&X and the Little Miami might impose, which is not to be sold without their consent, and upon the termination of the Lease is to revert to the Little Miami.

THE D&W also exists as a separate corporation. The Little Miami at the time of the Lease had taken up a part of the $738,000 of six per cent and seven per cent bonds. The Lessee also picked up the bonds from time to time and before their maturity in 1905 redeemed $32,000 that remained outstanding. They were all surrendered to the Little Miami and the mortgage was cancelled. Unfortunately, some careless holder lost three coupons, and the Little Miami has ever since been required by order of court to keep a suspense account of $90 to cash them. Some day the Little Miami will call on the D&W for a deed to all its property, and the D&W will go out of existence. Awaiting that day, the stockholders—the Little Miami owning a vast majority of the shares—are called to meet once a year in the Union Station at Dayton, and elect a board of thirteen directors.

The D&W owns a lease of 4.16 miles of road in Indiana between the state line and Richmond. The Little Miami, as lessee of the D&W, is bound to supply the money for the rent payable to the Richmond & Miami. After the Lease, the Lessee paid $5,500 to the Little Miami, who paid $5,500 to the D&W, who paid $5,500 to the R&M. The Lessee bought in the R&M, and after that the same $5,500 eventually came back home from its travels to the Lessee. The Lessee finally suggested that all the payments hither and yon be cleared, so that the money no longer passes around in a circle.

THE SURPLUS of the Little Miami, aggregating $949,450, in December, 1869, went to the Lessee. The directors, born of a generation that did not believe that unbalanced budgets bring prosperity, started from scratch to pile up another surplus out of unspent income. From 1870 to 1889, $400,350 was saved. In 23 more years, the surplus grew $347,450 in amount. The yearly increase since 1912 has been less, because the income from investments has been used to pay increased dividends.

The principal items credited to surplus in December, 1936, were: an annual payment of $21,500 by the Pennsylvania, capitalized at $430,000, being the par value of certain bonds which were not refunded in 1912; $54,000 of bonds and 2,116 shares, or $105,800 in par value of stock of the Little Miami itself; and securities of a general investment character costing $340,000. The total book value was $1,030,849.56.

BONDS

At the time of the Lease, the funded dept of the Little Miami, not assumed by the Lessee, was:
1. $100,000 six per cent Cincinnati Loan, made May 1, 1844, due December 31, 1880, secured by first mortgage; and
2. $1,480,000 six per cent Mortgage Bonds issued in 1853, due May 2, 1883.

The Cincinnati Loan was paid to the Cincinnati Sinking Fund Trustees by the Little Miami out of its surplus funds, and the mortgage was cancelled by the mayor. The Lessee, however, under Section 9 of the Lease, continued paying $6,000 each year to the Little Miami, until the Agreement of May 1, 1899, when the Lessee paid $100,000 in cash to the Little Miami.

The six per cent Mortgage Bonds of 1853 were extended from 1882 to November 2, 1912, by Renewal Mortgage 30-year five per cent bonds, secured by a general mortgage to Julius Dexter, Trustee, and guaranteed as to interest by the Lessee and the Pennsylvania. The Cincinnati banks did not bid enough for these bonds, and $1,233,000 were sold to Kuhn, Loeb & Co. of New York at 101, while the rest were exchanged for the old 1853 bonds. The directors of the Little Miami, in the hope that to him who asketh shall be given, set up a claim that the Lessee should pay six per cent regardless of the actual interest rate. The question was put to arbitration and the award, as might be expected, was that the Lessee was not liable for more than the interest really paid.

The capital stock remaining unissued in 1889 was not sufficient to pay the cost of betterments, and on January 28, 1890, $3,000,000 of 40-year seven per cent bonds, secured by second mortgage to the Cincinnati Safe Deposit Company and convertible at the option of the holder into stock, were authorized. $714,000 of these bonds were immediately turned over to the Lessee in settlement of the betterment account.

On the return of prosperity after the hard times

of the Nineties, the Little Miami authorized $3,000,-000 50-year three and one-half per cent Betterment Bonds dated May 1, 1901, secured by second mortgage to The Central Trust Company. The Lessee traded its $714,000 of seven per cent bonds with the coupons attached for the new issue. Through the six years up to 1907, $1,708,000 more were issued for betterments. The entire outstanding issue of $2,422,-000 was exchanged in 1908 for Special Guaranteed Betterment shares, and the mortgage was cancelled.

Upon maturity in 1912 of the Renewal Mortgage bonds of 1882, the Little Miami authorized $10,000,-000 50-year four per cent General Mortgage bonds, maturing November 1, 1962, secured by mortgage of all its properties to The Central Trust Company. $1,070,000 of Series A were issued to refund an equal amount of Renewal Mortgage bonds. The Little Miami bought in $474,000 of these with its own surplus funds from 1884 to 1912, and under the Agreement of April 9, 1907, the Lessee, instead of issuing new bonds for $430,000, has paid five per cent on the principal amount, or $21,500 yearly, to the Little Miami as additional rent. The balance of $44,000 was exchanged for new bonds and the Little Miami has since bought in $10,000 more. The bonds of Series A are listed on the New York Stock Exchange.

In 1936, $5,000,000 more, designated as Series B four per cent General Mortgage bonds, were issued to the Lessee in payment on account of betterments.

On December 31, 1936, the total funded debt of the Little Miami was $6,070,000 (less $54,000 held by the Little Miami) of four per cent bonds maturing

November 1, 1962, secured by General Mortgage on all its assets and guaranteed as to interest by the Lessee and the Pennsylvania Railroad.

CAPITAL STOCK

THE ORIGINAL 8.6% SHARES are the same as those provided for in 1836 by the charter. On December 1, 1869, 72,000 shares of the par value of $50 each, were authorized and 71,448, or $3,572,400 in par value, had been issued. The outstanding stock of the Columbus & Xenia aggregated $1,786,200.

Section 6 of the Lease requires the Lessee to pay rent enough for eight per cent dividends on six millions stock. The Little Miami was thereby able to pay eight per cent dividends on its own shares and on the shares of the C&X, and still have $51,312 left over for dividends on 12,828 shares which had never been issued. This was, in the parlance of today, gravy. The capital stock was increased, and 10,712 shares (of which two were never claimed) were distributed among stockholders in a 15 per cent stock dividend declared March 10, 1870. The remaining 2,116 shares, of the par value of $105,000, were withheld, and the Little Miami gets the eight per cent thereon.

14,586 shares, or $729,300 out of the five million dollars authorized, were issued to the Lessee for betterments from August, 1872, to June, 1882. The balance of 1,136 shares, in spite of a recommendation of a Joint Committee in 1906 that they be sold, still remain unissued.

On February 5, 1890, the capital stock was increased from $5,000,000 to $8,000,000, with a proviso that the new shares should be issued only for betterments or in exchange for convertible betterment bonds.

Eight per cent dividends have been paid on the Original shares every year since December, 1869. In January, 1897, Briggs S. Cunningham electrified a sleepy meeting of directors by proposing that the income from the invested surplus, which was by that time $563,300, be used to fatten the regular dividend by two-fifths of one per cent. Only three directors voted "Yes." Three years later the surplus had grown to $823,934, and Cunningham renewed his motion to pay ten cents more per share in December and another ten cents in June. Some of the directors still stood pat, but the motion carried. On November 28, 1913, the dividend was again increased by a third ten cents, payable in September. Since then, the regular annual dividend on the Original shares has been at the rate of eight and six-tenths per cent.

Of the 96,746 Original shares outstanding, 12,010 were held in 1936 by the Pennsylvania and 84,736 by 1436 shareholders. They grow in number year by year. Many shares are inherited by women who have apparently been warned never, never, under any circumstances, to sell their Little Miami. Since 1935, the Original shares have been listed on the Cincinnati Stock Exchange.

THE SPECIAL GUARANTEED BETTERMENT SHARES are also $50 par value, and have full voting rights. The dividend, however, is limited to four per cent, paid quarterly on the same days as the Original shares.

The Agreement of April 9, 1907, amended Section 10 of the Lease by providing that the Lessee might have the option of taking, in payment for betterments, either four per cent bonds or shares. On January 29, 1907, the stockholders voted for $2,000,000 of new shares in addition to the $3,000,000 authorized in February, 1890, and designated the entire five millions as Special Guaranteed Betterment stock to bear four per cent dividends, and to be issued only in payment for betterments.

Under the Agreement of April 9, 1907, the Lessee converted all the bonds received for betterments between 1890 and 1907, for 44,480 Special Guaranteed Betterment shares. The remainder, $2,578,000 in par value, has been issued to the Lessee from time to time, and at the end of 1936, was all outstanding.

An overwhelming majority of the Special Guaranteed Betterment shares are held by the Lessee or its associates. Besides these, there were in December, 1936, only 537 other holders. The shares have been listed since 1935 on the Cincinnati Stock Exchange.

ALTOGETHER, the Little Miami securities are the bluest of the blue-chips. Mighty few American investments have paid without let up for ninety-four years. The capital charges against the properties are much less than their actual value, so that if the Little Miami were ever called on to operate its road again, it would undoubtedly earn enough for interest and dividends. The Lessee is bound to pay the rental before it can even pay the interest on its own bonds, and this obligation is guaranteed by the greatest railroad in the world. The Pennsylvania will never, as long as it exists, give up its line to Cincinnati and its principal connection with the South.

The stock and bonds of the Little Miami outstanding at the end of 1936 were:

	Four Per Cent General Mortgage Bonds Series A Due 11/2/1962	Four Per Cent General Mortgage Bonds Series B Due 11/2/1962	Original Stock	Special Guaranteed Betterment Stock	Totals
Issued to the public	$1,016,000	—0—	$4,037,050	—0—	$5,053,050
Issued for Betterments to the Lessee	—0—	$5,000,000	$ 800,250	$5,000,000	$10,800,250
Held by the Little Miami	$ 54,000	—0—	$ 105,800	—0—	$ 159,800
Totals	$1,070,000	$5,000,000	$4,943,100	$5,000,000	$16,013,100

DIRECTORS

Since the Lease, little more has been required of the directors than a knowledge of finance, some business acumen and an allowance of common sense. Pleasant association with other gentlemen, and, as may be noticed, an unusual longevity are the rewards of the service rendered.

Men respected and honored in the city have been glad to go on the Board. To name all who deserve mention would make a tedious list; instead, only a few may be picked out here for passing attention.

Henry Hanna, who came from Pittsburgh in 1846, trained for the law, but with greater experience in business and finance, was Vice-President in 1875 and was promoted to President in 1884. He resigned January 28, 1890, to stay on until 1905 as a member of the Board. Upon his death, his associates spoke feelingly of his service of fifty years as a director, officer and member of many committees, all without salary or other compensation, but always with "wisdom, rare ability and faithfulness."

Frank J. Jones went on the Board in 1884, a gallant young Civil War veteran. Graduate of Yale, he left the Harvard Law School in April of 1861 to enlist in the 6th O.V.I., fought at Shiloh, served as aide-de-camp and Assistant Inspector General and left the army with the rank of Major brevet. He became President in 1890, and spent thirty-seven useful years in that position until his death on June 6, 1927.

Henry C. Urner was Secretary from the annual meeting in February, 1892, and carried on for 16 years. Charles D. Jones followed Urner as Secretary, served twenty years and succeeded his father as President. He lived seven years longer and died in office October 24, 1935, to the regret of all those who knew him.

William Worthington, one of the ablest lawyers that ever practiced in Cincinnati, was director for thirty-nine years and General Counsel for thirty-three. "No other man possessed such an intimate knowledge of its early history."

Learner B. Harrison, wholesale grocer from pioneer days until the Civil War and thereafter banker until his death at 89 in 1902, was on the Board for thirty years. His son, Charles L. Harrison, went on the Board in 1908, and was President at his death in 1936.

Briggs S. Cunningham was a director twenty-two years, while James N. Gamble of Procter & Gamble resigned because of old age after forty years.

Charles P. Taft, following in the footsteps of his father, was a director for thirty-seven years until his death at the end of 1929.

Of the present directors, Louis J. Hauck has filled out his thirty-third year.

Distinguished officers of the Pennsylvania Railroad have served with the Board since 1914, beginning with Edward B. Taylor and J. J. Turner. In 1936, the group was led by that fine gentleman, A. J. County, Vice-President in charge of finance and corporate relations, and with him were H. E. Newcomet, Vice-President in charge of lines west of Columbus, George J. Adams, Chief of Corporate Work, and Robert C. Barnard, General Agent and Superintendent at Cincinnati.

www.ingramcontent.com/pod-product-compliance
Lightning Source LLC
Chambersburg PA
CBHW030325100526
44592CB00010B/571